Case Management
An Introduction to Concepts and Skills,
Second Edition

Arthur J. Frankel
University of North Carolina, Wilmington

Sheldon R. Gelman
Schachne Dean and Professor
Wurzweiler School of Social Work
Yeshiva University

D0166556

LYCEUM
BOOKS, INC.

Chicago, Illinois

Published by
Lyceum Books, Inc.
5758 S. Blackstone Avenue
Chicago, Illinois 60637
773-643-1902 (phone)
773-643-1903 (fax)
http://www.lyceumbooks.com

Library of Congress Cataloging-in-Publication Data
Frankel, Arthur J., 1944–
    Case Management : an introduction to concepts and skills /
    Arthur J. Frankel, Sheldon R. Gelman.—2nd ed.
        p.   cm.
    Includes bibliographical references and index.
    ISBN 0-925065-74-9 (pbk. : alk paper)
        1. Social case work.   I. Gelman, Sheldon.   II. Title
HV43.F695   2004
    361.3'2—dc22   2003020503

Contents

Notes on the Authors

SHELDON R. GELMAN is professor and Dorothy and David I. Schachne Dean at the Wurzweiler School of Social Work of Yeshiva University in New York. He also serves the university as associate vice president for academic affairs. Formerly a professor in and director of the social work program at Pennsylvania State University, he earned his bachelor's degree in psychology and his master's degree in social group work at the University of Pittsburgh. He received his Ph.D. in welfare planning from the Heller School of Brandeis University and his M.S.L. (master of studies in law) from Yale University Law School.

Dr. Gelman is a member of the Academy of Certified Social Workers and the Academy of Mental Retardation and a Fellow of the American Association on Mental Retardation. He has published numerous articles dealing with the impact of legislation and policies on the delivery of social services.

He has held office and served on national commissions and on the boards of the Council of Social Work Education (CSWE), the American Association on Mental Retardation (AAMR), and the National Association of Social Workers (NASW). Dr. Gelman serves as a consultant and staff development resource to a range of public and voluntary social welfare organizations interested in improving the quality of their services and in developing procedures and practices that reduce liability exposure.

ARTHUR J. FRANKEL, M.S.W., Ph.D., received his master's in groupwork in 1970 and a joint doctorate in social work and psychology in 1972, both from the University of Michigan. He has taught at the University of Louisville and Rutgers University and currently is a professor in the school of social work at University of North Carolina, Wilmington. He has written many publications relating to case management and has conducted extensive case management research in the areas of child welfare, the homeless, and forensic social work.

Preface to the Second Edition

We are pleased that the first edition of this book has been so well received and that the use and application of case management practice has grown and matured. The second edition has been enhanced with expanded and updated references and new sections on case management with the homeless and those afflicted with HIV/AIDS. A new chapter 9 on the challenges and visions of case management in the future replaces the brief discussion on caseloads, supervision, and continuing education. Additional exercises for instructors or trainers have been added to chapters 2, 3, 4, 6, 7, 8, and 9.

Preface to the First Edition

This book is designed to be used wherever students or human service workers are being trained in case management methods. Such training can be found in senior-year BSW college programs, first-year MSW programs, nursing schools, and criminal justice programs. This text is meant to augment more general texts in undergraduate and graduate education, in order to focus more intensively on case management roles, process, and specific skills that students will need both in their internships and later as professionals. This book should also be of significant help to agencies that train workers in case management through in-service workshops, seminars, and other short-term programs. Such types of training occur in child welfare, addiction, mental health, hospital, and criminal justice settings.

The skill-based chapters are followed by suggestions for optional exercises that teachers and trainers may use to help students practice requisite skills. Teaching and training methods differ considerably, and there are literally thousands of ways to teach case management skills effectively. The purpose of the optional exercise section is simply to offer a few suggestions for teachers, who need all the support they can get in the complex process of case management education.

This book is written with attention to case management as an art and as a science. Many references are cited for those who wish to pursue specific aspects of case management. The book also focuses on case management "practice wisdom," which is essential to the development of practice skills in social services. We hope that this style of presentation, along with the exercises at the end of the skill chapters, will help make your case management training meaningful, enjoyable, and even inspirational.

From Arthur J. Frankel:

I would like to thank my coauthor, Sheldon Gelman, with whom it was a pleasure to work. I would also like to acknowledge my daughter, Rachel Elise Frankel, who helped inspire me to write this book, and to express my appreciation to my wife, Marylou McCarthy, MSW, LCSW, who supported me in the process.

From Sheldon R. Gelman:

Collaborating with my colleague, Arthur Frankel, has been an interesting experience in part because our styles of writing and knowledge bases complement each other. Appreciation to my wife, Ilene S. Gelman, ACSW, who commented on drafts of each chapter.

Part 1
Case Management Practice

1 The Evolution of Case Management Practice

What Is Case Management?

Case management as a way of helping people has a long and rich history. At the very beginnings of social work, in the settlement house days in New York and Chicago, social workers guided families needing help into existing private and public support networks, meager though they might have been. When resources were not readily available, social workers helped mobilize their communities for social action. They effectively lobbied for new and innovative ways to support the poor, the infirm, immigrants, families, and children. Today we may talk about generalist practice, the systems approach, methods of casework, groupwork, community organization, and various practice theories, but a rose by any other name is still a rose. The history of social work is filled with practitioners who worked with their clients using the same case management methods used today—they just didn't call it case management.

Over the last thirty years, the term "case management" has been widely applied to describe a process or method of service delivery and a set of roles assumed by service providers. Case management approaches have been utilized in medical or health care facilities, with elderly clients, substance abusers, the chronically mentally ill, the developmentally disabled, AIDS patients, inmates released from prisons, child welfare cases, employment training and employee assistance programs, and with populations at risk.

Case management, which is sometimes referred to as "clinical case management," "service coordination," or "comprehensive psychosocial enhancement," has two essential and often conflicting purposes: (1) improving the quality of care to vulnerable populations, and (2) controlling the costs of such care. While the focus of case management is linking a client to needed services, other elements involve advocacy and social action (Ballew & Mink, 1997).

Historically, there have been many definitions of case management. Generically, it is a way of helping people identify the areas where they need help and connecting them to the personal and community resources that will help them (Rubin, 1992). It is a systematic problem-solving process that enables and facilitates individuals in their interaction with their environment. According to the National Association of Social Workers (1984), "Case management is a mechanism for ensuring a comprehensive program that will meet an individual's need for care by coordinating and linking components of a service delivery system." According to Dinerman (1992), "It is a function designed to arrange for, and to sequence, needed services of different sorts by various providers on behalf of a client or client family." Case management involves the engagement of a client in a system of services by an accountable professional. According to the American Association on Mental Retardation (1994), "Service coordination (case management) is an ongoing process that consists of the assessment of wants and needs, planning, locating and securing supports and services, monitoring and follow-along. The individual or family is the defining force of the service coordination process." In the words of the National Conference on Social Welfare (1981), "Case management is a growing, evolving process which is shaped by forces in the environment in which it exists." The National Association of Social Workers views case management as the link between the client and the service delivery system (1992). One can see from these definitions that case management is the glue that binds a fragmented array of services to the unique and changing needs of clients.

Case managers become experts on community resources that might help their clients, including government entitlements, charities, job openings, education, child care, legal aid, housing, transportation, and recreational opportunities. Case managers know the procedures clients need to follow in applying for and receiving help. Sometimes, when necessary services are not available, case managers initiate strategies to help communities develop new resources and systems for their clients.

Effective case management requires that a comprehensive and coordinated array of appropriate services be available and accessible within a realistic and appropriate time frame. Without such a system, case management is only an administrative tool that manages clients' access to services. Case management is not just a linking mechanism, but a principle that guides the provision of a full range of needed services. Unfortunately, service networks rarely meet this level of expectation. While case management is conceived as one component of a comprehensive care system, it is not seen as a way to fix an inadequate or incomplete system of care. As Moore notes, "the notion that case management is a mechanism for the coordination of services is a myth that has been used to rationalize the current state of fragmentation . . . and becomes a mechanism for rationing services" (Moore, 1992). Case management is an effective tool, but not a panacea for spanning organizational boundaries (Jansson, 2003).

If the goal is service access and coordination, the case manager's efforts are designed to alleviate or counter the fragmentation of services and the natural tendency of bureaucratic organizations toward disorganization. For the case manager to achieve this goal, the following elements or conditions must be present:

- an accurate assessment and ongoing evaluation of client needs;

- the ability to link clients to resources appropriate to their needs;

- the power to ensure that appropriate and needed services are actually delivered;

- the capacity to see that services are utilized;

- a commitment to evaluating the impacts and outcomes of interventions.

If the goal of case management is seen only as cost containment, or a "least change" alternative, then the focal point of intervention becomes one of the systematic management and processing of individuals rather than one of engaging clients in a process. There is a difference between case management practice that contributes to the implementation of a service plan, and case management systems that represent the administrative structure and interagency networks in which the case manager functions. One must also distinguish between case management models that are client-driven and those that are provider-driven. The former, based on a strengths perspective closely linked to an empowerment model, include active client engagement (see Rapp, 1997; Saleeby, 1992, 1997; Tice & Perkins, 1998). The latter are more clerical and bureaucratic, with a focus on documentation.

Managed Care vs. Case Management

Managed care, unlike case management, is a practice or method of financing and delivering services to a range of populations. Although it involves some of the concepts and activities of case management, the two approaches have different objectives. Activities associated with managed care are designed to reduce costs by discouraging unnecessary or expensive services. Case management, with its focus on linking clients to services, tries to obtain the most appropriate and cost-effective help for them. Managed care programs review and intervene in decisions about what services are provided, influence or limit who the provider will be, and predetermine the payment for the provider.

Managed care systems, which include health maintenance organizations (HMOS), point-of-service plans (PSPs), and preferred provider arrangements (PPOs), have come to dominate the delivery of health care in this country. They are also the primary method of financing mental-health and substance-abuse services and are rapidly becoming the way public agencies contract with private organizations that provide specialized services for children and the elderly. Managed care plans are characterized by the following: A preauthorization requirement to qualify for a particular service; precertification for a given type or amount of service; concurrent review of the service and the client's response; utilization review and discharge-planning procedures; prospective pricing; service bundling; network development; peer review; and a capitation system of payment. While case managers need to be aware of the all enveloping managed care environment, it is not the authors' intent to focus on managed care in this volume. For those interested in expanding their knowledge and skill in this area, we suggest the following resources: Cohen, 2003; Corcoran & Vandiver, 1996; Dziegielewski, 1998; Edinburg & Cottler, 1995; Franklin, 2002; Gibelman, 2002; Jackson, 1995; Mizrahi, 1993; National Association of Social Workers, 1993; Perloff, 1996; Schames & Lightburn, 1998; Shera, 1996; Strom-Gottfried, 1997; Winegar, 1996.

Who Does Case Management, and in What Settings?

Most social workers who specialize in direct practice do case management. Generalist practitioners, caseworkers, and groupworkers work with clients in the structured ways associated with their respective modalities, usually in weekly sessions over a number of weeks or months, directly trying to help using the theoretical practice model of their choice. However, in order to be of maximum help in either a casework or groupwork context, most social workers look beyond their offices into the social and community context in which their clients live. In other words, they help clients understand their problems as part of a broader systems approach and help them intervene accordingly.

The major differences between generalist practice, the specialized methods of social work practice, and case management are those of degree. All involve conducting extensive assessments (psycho-socials); all develop goals and intervention plans; and all work toward termination when clients reach their goals. Case managers tend to emphasize the use of community resources to help clients meet their needs. Intervention is viewed in terms of facilitation, connecting clients to the agencies, social service organizations, governmental entities, educational institutions, community organizations, and key people that can help them. It is common for one of these referrals to be to an agency that offers specialized casework or groupwork services. Ongoing case management contacts with clients usually revolve around making sure that the service plan and the community connections are functioning, augmenting them if necessary. Unfortunately, agency-based caseworkers and groupworkers often lack the time to perform necessary case management services with their clients. They rely on professional case managers who have much more time and expertise, working in tandem with them to connect clients to services in the community.

Although it is clear that social work is heavily involved in case management training and services, the profession does not own the field. The need for professionals who can identify and manage the vast array of services is widespread. For example, case managers in the medical profession may include nurses, occupational therapists, medical assistants, and nutritionists (see Cesta & Tahan, 2003). Professionals may also act as case managers in the legal profession, especially legal aid. In fact, any agency that uses psychiatry or psychology, or marriage or family counseling may employ non–social work staff to act as case managers.

Where Does Case Management Training Occur?

Professional social workers receive their case management training in BSW and MSW programs in schools of social work. Case management training also takes place in nursing schools, other schools connected with the medical profession, junior-college associate degree programs in social work, and services involving welfare, foster care, criminal justice, drug treatment, mental illness, and the elderly. Thousands of social service workers who perform case management functions are trained through their ongoing supervision, workshops, and continuing education programs. According to the National Association of Social Workers, the social work case manager shall:

1. Have a baccalaureate or graduate degree from a social work program accredited by the Council on Social Work Education and shall possess the knowledge, skill, and experience necessary to competently perform case management activities.

2. Use his or her professional skills and competence to serve the client whose interests are of primary concern.

3. Ensure that clients are involved in all phases of case management practice to the greatest extent possible.

4. Ensure the client's right to privacy and ensure appropriate confidentiality when information about the client is released to others.

5. Intervene at the client level to provide and/or coordinate the delivery of direct services to clients and their families.

6. Intervene at the service systems level to support existing case management services and to expand the supply of and improve access to needed services.

7. Be knowledgeable about resource availability, service costs, and budgetary parameters and be fiscally responsible in carrying out all case management functions and activities.

8. Participate in evaluative and quality assurance activities designed to monitor the appropriateness and effectiveness of both the service delivery system in which case management operates as well as the case manager's own case management services, and to otherwise ensure full professional accountability.

9. Carry a reasonable caseload that allows the case manager to effectively plan, provide, and evaluate case management tasks related to client and system interventions.

10. Treat colleagues with courtesy and respect and strive to enhance interprofessional, intraprofessional, and interagency cooperation on behalf of the client.
(National Association of Social Workers, 1992)

The National Association of Case Management (NACM) was founded in 1990. Its purpose is to provide case managers and other community support professionals with opportunities for professional growth. The organization accomplishes its goals through educational meetings, symposia, and the dissemination of materials relating to the case management process. The National Academy of Certified Case Managers (NACCM), which has a heavy nursing orientation, was created to assure competence in the performance of case management functions through a validated standardized examination. The American Case Management Association (ACMA), an association of nurses and social workers, advocates for case management practice in hospitals and the health system. The Case Management Society of America (CMSA) issued standards for case managers in 1998. The Center for Case Mangement (CMM) has a certification and credentialing program for case management administrators, the CMAC. A CCM is offered by the Commission for Case Management Certification (CCMC), and the National Association of Social Workers offers certification at two levels, the certified social work case manager (CSWCM) and the certified advanced social work case manager (C-ACSWCM). The *Journal of Case Management* and the *Case Management Journal* are quarterly publications that offer professional forums for presentations on case management issues and practices. Some universities also offer "certificates in case management" for individuals preparing to work in various state-funded programs that have a mandated case management component. These programs are available to individuals who have bachelor's or advanced degrees in social work, nursing, or other health/human service professions. A master's degree in case management is even available online via distance-learning courses and experiential learning.

Case Management Client Populations

Every client population group can profit from case management services. In fact, current social work theory suggests that almost every client would benefit if the case management method were part of his or her service intervention plan. Be that as it may, case management is a major focus of service delivery systems in many areas, while in others it is integrated with other service methods.

Children's services and public welfare are two major domains for case management practice. Every state maintains departments that use case management—early intervention programs, foster care, child protective services, welfare, child care, housing, food distribution, employment, and job training. Many case managers are involved with the chronic mentally ill and the addicted. The criminal justice system utilizes case management in prisons, halfway houses, and programs that offer prevention and alternatives to incarceration. Mental-health settings, both in institutions and in the community, have case management staff to augment other types of direct services, such as clinical casework and psychiatry. Programs dealing with individuals who are developmentally disabled or autistic make heavy use of case management, as do programs for the aged. Another large domain for case management is in medical settings, such as hospitals and community health agencies (see Cesta & Tahan, 2003; Snowden, 2003).

Even agencies that do not identify case managers as such often assume that workers will integrate case management into their practice. This is particularly true in the fields of community mental health and family service, which employ clinical social workers to offer case management services in the private sector. For example, one can find social workers specializing in geriatric work being privately employed by families to find housing and other support services for their elderly relatives; or workers in the area of developmental disabilities hired to search for appropriate and affordable housing for children or young adults who need to be placed out of their homes. The opportunities for case management practice in the newly emerging managed care marketplace are also significantly increasing for social work professionals.

2 Overview of Case Management Practice

Systems Theory

While there are some differences between case management and other methods of social work, there is one overriding theoretical theme that unifies case management with the rest of social work—systems theory. The basic idea behind systems theory is quite simple: People's behavior and attitudes are affected by everything and everyone around them. They are affected by their families, friends, and relatives; their jobs, educational experience, and educational opportunities; how much money they have and how they spend it. Age, gender, race, religion, ethnic identity, sexual preference, and political ideology affect people, as do the house and community in which they live, their health and access to health services, the government under which they live, and the recreational and community services available to them.

Any problem an individual faces is not a factor only of his or her unique psychological makeup. It is a combination of many forces working on a person that has brought her or him to the point of voluntarily seeking or being mandated to receive help. Thus the solution to anyone's problems, including our own, must be seen in the context of many different levels of intervention. In order to pull yourself up by the bootstraps, you need more than the motivation to reach for your shoes. You may need help finding a decent pair of shoes, learning how to put them on, learning how to walk, or having someplace meaningful to walk to. You may find that some people are hoarding shoes, making it harder for you to find them. Maybe the only shoes available are cheap ones that fall apart. Maybe you find that shoe stores are

Intervention Focus Areas in Case Management Practive

	Micro	Mezzo	Macro
Direct Interventions	*With Clients*	*With Clients*	*With Clients*
Outreach Interventions	*On Behalf of Clients*	*On Behalf of Clients*	*On Behalf of Clients*

closed to you, perhaps because of your schooling, your race, or your sex.

Case managers use the concept of systems theory in very practical ways. We divide up potential assessment areas into three levels: personal/interpersonal areas, called the "micro" level; institutional/ organizational/community issues, called the "mezzo" level; and social policy/governmental/cultural issues, called the "macro" level. Interventions also take into account each of these three levels; a systems approach to case management assumes that worker behavior combines interventions in all three domains. Additionally, interventions in each of these areas could be directly with clients—*direct interventions*—or with others on behalf of clients—*indirect, or outreach interventions.*

Thus, there is a two-by-three practice case management systems matrix covering the practice of every case management program (Frankel & Heft-LaPorte, 1998). For example, a worker in the micro domain could provide short-term crisis intervention services (direct) and make a referral to an agency for therapy (outreach). In the mezzo area, a worker might help clients form a community support group (direct) and make a contract with a new agency for client referrals (outreach). In the macro domain, a worker could organize clients to help with voter registration (direct) and work with an NASW committee to lobby for changes in the welfare law (outreach). It is rare for a case management program to focus on all three of these possible practice domains; most programs focus on one or two. We will be looking at these issues more intensively as we move into the practice of case management.

Case Management Functions

In order to function effectively as a case manager, you should have an understanding of general case management functions, models, and tasks. Rose and Moore have identified the following case management functions:

> (1) outreach to or identification of clients, (2) assessment of needs, (3) service or treatment planning, (4) linking or referring clients to appropriate resources, and (5) monitoring cases to ensure that services are delivered and used. (Rose & Moore, 1995)

An expanded and more detailed set of case management functions is provided by Moore:

- to assess the individual's ability to meet environmental challenges;
- to assess the caring capability of the individual's family and primary group;
- to assess the resources within the formal system of care;
- to enable individuals to use their personal resources in meeting environmental challenges;
- to enable families and primary groups to expand their caretaking capacity;
- to facilitate effective negotiation by individuals for resources from families or primary groups and formal service providers;
- to facilitate effective interchanges between families or primary groups and the formal system of care;
- to evaluate the ongoing needs of the individual;
- to evaluate the extent to which the individual is adequately supported by both the family or primary group and the formal system of care;
- to evaluate the extent to which the efforts of the family or primary group are integrated with those of the formal care system.

(Moore, 1990)

For these functions to be performed effectively, the case manager must possess knowledge and expertise relating to both social systems and the etiology, needs, and functioning of the client/ consumer. The case manager also needs the interpersonal skills not only to assess the needs and circumstances of the client accurately but also to engage him or her in the process so that both can agree on what is to be done. Although the case manager might be able only to mitigate insufficiencies in the service network, he or she must have sufficient power and authority to make things happen (Rubin, 1992). Workers must also have caseloads of a reasonable size, lest they become processors rather than facilitators or enablers.

Case Management Models

Several models of case management have been identified by various authors; Levine and Fleming (1985) have developed the following classification scheme for case management models:

- generalist
- specialist
- therapist
- family
- psychosocial rehabilitation
- supportive
- volunteer

More recently, Bachrach (1989); Bond, Miller, Krumwied, & Ward (1988); Bush, Langord, Rosen, & Gott (1990); and Kanter (1989, 1991) have used the following terms to describe case management models:

- assertive
- intensive
- rehabilitation-oriented
- development/acquisition
- strengths
- clinical.

Eggert, Friedman, and Zimmer (1990) have identified three intensive case management models: the home health care team, the neighborhood team, and a centralized individual model. These models differ in terms of the nature of client assessment and re-assessment involved, the kind of direct services provided, and whether crisis intervention is available or utilized. Rothman (1991, 1994) proposes another model of case management that contains the following fifteen sequentially linked functions: access (outreach and referral), intake, assessment, goal setting, intervention planning, resource identification and indexing, formal linkage (agencies and programs), informal linkage (social network), monitoring, reassessment, outcome evaluation, interagency coordination, counseling, therapy, advocacy. Rothman (2002) categorizes the first eleven of these functions as sequential and the later four as intermittent.

The type of case management model used and the degree, level, and extent of case management activities required will vary depending on the needs and level of functioning of the individual. Authors like Gilson (1998), Rapp (1997), Saleeby (1992, 1997); and Tice and Perkens (1998) stress the need to develop models that recognize and build on client strengths. The model is also dependent on the overall case management goal and the level of skills of the manager. Some individuals will require intensive and ongoing attention. Others will require ongoing but less intensive involvement. Some will need only limited or short-term assistance, while others will require minimal monitoring. Your goal is to balance the client's needs and capabilities with a range of formal and informal supports and resources.

Case Management Tasks

Probably the most comprehensive listing of tasks required of and performed by case managers was developed by Bertsche and Horejsi in 1980. The thirteen basic tasks provide a clear and concise description of case management responsibilities:

1. Complete the initial interviews with the client and his or her family to assess the client's eligibility for services.

2. Gather relevant and useful data from the client, family, or other agencies, and so on to formulate a psychosocial assessment of the client and his or her family.

3. Assemble and guide group discussions and decision-making sessions among relevant professionals and program representatives, the client and his or her family, and significant others to formulate goals and design an integrated intervention plan.

4. Monitor adherence to the plan and manage the flow of accurate information within the action system to maintain a goal orientation and coordination momentum.

5. Provide "follow-along" to the client and his or her family to speed identification of unexpected problems in service delivery and to serve as a general troubleshooter on behalf of the client.

6. Provide counseling and information to help the client and his or her family in situations of crisis and conflict with service providers.

7. Provide ongoing emotional support to the client and his or her family so they can cope better with problems and utilize professionals and complex services.

8. Complete the necessary paperwork to maintain documentation of client progress and adherence to the plan by all concerned.

9. Act as a liaison between the client and his or her family and all relevant professionals, programs, and informal resources involved in the overall intervention plan to help the client make his or her preferences known and secure the services needed.

10. Act as a liaison between programs, providing services to the client to ensure the smooth flow of information and minimize the conflict between the subsystems.

11. Establish and maintain credibility and good public relations with significant formal and informal resource systems to mobilize resources for current and future clients.

12. Perform effectively and as a "good bureaucrat" within the organization to be in a position to develop and modify policies and procedures affecting clients and the effectiveness of the service delivery system.

13. Secure and maintain the respect and support of those in positions of authority so their influence can be enlisted on behalf of the client and used, when necessary, to encourage other individuals and agencies to participate in the coordination effort.

(Bertsche & Horejsi, 1980)

For other listings of case management tasks, see Grube & Chernesky, 2001; Mather & Hull, 2002; Rothman, 2002; and Vourlekis & Green, 1992.

Confidentiality Issues

Before going any further, we need to deal with the very basic ethical and legal issue of confidentiality. There are very clear guidelines in social work and other helping professions about what information case managers can share about their clients. Using the Social Work Code of Ethics as an example, the guidelines insist that clients have a right to know who will have access to their records and the information in them. No information about a client is supposed to be shared outside the worker-client relationship without the express, and usually written, consent of the client (National Association of Social Workers, 1996). The issues of privacy and confidentiality have taken on added importance as the provisions of the Health Insurance Portability and Accounting Act (HIPAA) of 1996 took effect in April 2003. In the first contact with clients, issues relating to agency policies and the agency policy concerning confidentiality need to be discussed. Further work with clients cannot proceed unless they consent in writing to these policies, or at least show that they understand what the policies will be. In this way, clients can make informed decisions about what they will share with the worker.

When there is a legal mandate to share information with other professionals and agencies without clients' consent, they need to be told that this will occur. When clients are unable to understand policies concerning confidentiality—children or retarded citizens, for example—confidentiality is still to be respected and permission for release or sharing of information must be obtained from an authorized third party.

Case managers have always had a special problem when it comes to confidentiality, which is now further complicated when health information is involved (HIPAA Privacy Rule). By the very nature of the case management roles, they will be sharing information about clients with other agencies and professionals in the referral and advocacy process (Davidson & Davidson, 1996; Watkins, 1989). Case managers often receive personal information during meetings with clients, much the same as do caseworkers and therapists. Case management records, however, may also contain information collected from a wide variety of sources. What makes confidentiality a potential problem for case management is that some of this information may have to be shared with a broad spectrum of agencies and professionals in seeking out and making appropriate referrals. Caseworkers and other therapists who do individual counseling may also face these same issues, but not to the degree of a case manager, whose job is defined as the professional responsible for galvanizing the community on behalf of clients. Case managers have many more opportunities to share information about clients outside of their agency boundaries, and thus must be extremely vigilant to maintain confidentiality. Given the growing use of computerized record-keeping systems and HIPAA requirements, proactive safeguards must be utilized to limit access and to assure client confidentiality (Brannigan, 1992; Lawrence, 1994; Mills-Groninger, 2003). You must always remember to get permission from your clients in making contacts on their behalf if anything about them will be discussed, even if you only mention their names. If referral communications are mandated by law, clients still have the right to know under what conditions their names and case information will be shared (Kagel, 1993).

An important case management goal is to empower clients to case manage their own problems, to learn to "work the system" on their own behalf. When clients are initiating agency and professional contacts at a case manager's behest, they need to learn what their rights are when asked for potentially sensitive information about their lives. For example, clients are not required to acknowledge whether they are HIV-positive when applying to an agency for job training, employment, or housing. Similarly, people's sexual orientation is of no concern to any agency personnel if clients are requesting access to casework or groupwork services.

The Process of Case Management

The goals of case management are basically twofold. First, we need to help people connect to the personal, interpersonal, and community resources that will help them resolve their problems. Secondly, and just as important, we want to teach them how to become their own case managers—to be able to identify their needs and solve their problems independently. While this second goal may not always be achievable, it is a value for case managers to strive toward.

Social work in general, and case management in particular, follows a systematic process of working with people regardless of the types of clients or their problems. This process cuts across generalist, casework, groupwork, administration, and community organization methods, with workers using similar skills no matter what their practice orientation (see Ballew & Mink, 1997). This process does not always flow sequentially. It may proceed in cycles, returning to the beginning as the worker learns more about the client. The longer you work with clients, the more opportunity you have to identify additional problem areas or define problems in different contexts. As that happens, you will need to return to the problem-definition phase and continue through the case management process, adding depth and breadth to the assessment as time goes on.

Steps in the Case Management Process

- Defining the problem
- Determining the severity of the problem
- Developing hypotheses concerning *why* client problems are occurring

- Establishing goals
- Developing and implementing a service intervention plan
- Evaluating the success of service interventions
- Termination
- Follow-up

Each of these steps raises different issues and carries with it the need for specialized skills.

1. Defining the problem

The case management process starts with an information-gathering procedure called the *psycho-social*. Relatively systematic, it requires the worker to find out everything about a client and his or her life that could be relevant to problem solving. It covers questions that relate to micro, mezzo, and macro levels. Many agencies have standard forms to help case managers conduct psycho-socials; we will spend some time on this issue later in this handbook.

One of the essential pieces of information the case manager needs to establish is the problems that brought the client to the agency. Sometimes the problems are initially defined by the agency itself. For example, if you work in a child abuse agency, most of your clients will have abuse as a defined problem. Many agencies focus on particular areas that define clients' presenting problems before they are accepted for service.

However, since we know that every problem in life is connected to other problems and issues—part of the systems approach—it is likely that presenting problems are the proverbial tip of the iceberg. Frequently, clients with multiple problems end up at one particular agency simply by chance. Thus, to assume that presenting problems automatically define goals and service intervention plans is often unwarranted. For example, a homeless, chronically mentally ill, drug-addicted man who steals purses to support his habit could end up in any number of agencies—a homeless shelter, a mental health clinic, a psychiatric outpatient or inpatient hospital, a drug treatment program, or a forensic treatment program in jail.

Clients also have their own sense of why they need help. This is often true of those who arrive at an agency voluntarily, on their own or through professional referrals. Other clients are mandated to seek help, usually through the courts; their problems will be initially defined by where their "client career" started. The important thing to remember is that whatever the presenting problem may be, it is up to you, through the process of the psycho-social, to discover the entire gamut of possible problems in your clients' lives.

2. Determining the severity of the problem

During the process of the psycho-social, the case manager becomes aware of a series of possible client problems, many of course interconnected. It is important to determine how severe each of them is; the severity of a problem is a direct indication of how immediately it needs to be addressed.

In determining problem severity, case managers must take into consideration the opinions of their clients. Respect for clients' sense of themselves and their assessment of their own lives is at the center of social work's value system, and should not be taken lightly. A worker cannot help anyone effectively unless there is agreement about what problems need to be addressed. If there is disagreement, the issues need to be addressed and overcome, if possible, before moving on to the next step in the case management process.

3. Developing hypotheses concerning why client problems are occurring

Determining why a client has problems is one of the most difficult tasks facing the case manager. This task is sometimes called the assessment of controlling conditions, or "assessment" for short. Various theories that can aid you in this task include the behavioral approach, psychodynamic theories, organizational theory, community psychology theory, social psychology, and economic and political theory. As you become more sophisticated in case management, you may wish to study what some of these theories have to say about social ills in American society.

However, the basic underlying theory that will guide your assessment of controlling conditions is systems theory. You will be trying to understand how the interplay of forces from micro to macro is affecting your client. At the micro level, what role does the family play? What attempts have the client and family made to resolve the problem? What are the client and family strengths that can be drawn on to help? At the mezzo level, what agency, organizational, and community resources have been involved in trying to help? What blocks, if any, have been put in the client's way? What additional resources are available and why haven't they been used? At the macro level, what are the governmental policies and regulations that govern support for your client? How do ethnic, racial, and cultural factors play into the maintenance of client problems?

A good assessment should lead you and your clients into making hypotheses about what is causing their problems, further indicating the direction of service interventions. Assessment is useless unless it points to concrete solutions. In addition, assessments that lead to stereotypical "plug and chug" solutions should be avoided because they minimize individual differences. For example, if case management assessment always leads to suggesting therapy, why bother doing a psycho-social? While there are obviously times when therapy is necessary and appropriate, other interventions might do more to lift a person's spirit and sense of hope. Similarly, a client who is in need of mental health services but has not been successful in satisfying basic needs for food, shelter, or medical care, may not benefit from mental health services until the other needs are met. Each client offers a unique opportunity to assess controlling conditions leading to helpful interventions.

4. Establishing goals

The development of clear goals is a very important phase of the case management process. A goal is a statement defining the expected outcome for each client by the time case management services are terminated. Goal statements should include a time frame and a date by which the goal will be reached. A goal without a date opens the possibility for an endless service delivery process.

Within a given time frame, case management goals are stated

in terms of one or more of the following areas: (1) What are the behavior changes expected of the client? (2) What community agency social services is the client expected to be utilizing? (3) What economic, medical, or educational support services is the client expected to use? (4) What community/neighborhood support systems is the client likely to be a part of ? (5) What self-initiated problem-solving skills are expected of the client? A note of caution: case managers should be careful not to set goals that are unrealistic or unachievable or that do not call for clients to accept responsibility. Setting such goals may expose both the organization and the case manager to accusations that they have not delivered on promises, and may result in legal liability.

Whenever possible, goals for case management services should be established *with,* not *for,* each client. In most situations, clients need to be involved in the work of figuring out where they want to be at a given time. Of course the worker is an important resource in this process, suggesting options, offering opinions, discussing what might be reasonable and possible given the known resources, helping people focus, and, when appropriate, supporting clients who want to explore the development of new resources as one of their goals. Case management works *much* more effectively when clients are intensively involved in all stages of the process to the extent possible. Consumer involvement cannot be emphasized enough. People tend to work toward goals in which they feel they have had involvement; no one likes to have goals imposed on them without their cooperation and agreement. The client's investment in the process is critical. Even in case management programs where clients are mandated to receive service, such as child abuse or forensic programs, it is important that they subscribe to the goals and plans set with them. If this does not happen, a client's motivation to participate and complete service plans will be greatly weakened and the goals far less likely of attainment.

A case manager cannot collaborate in setting goals with all clients. Some will not cooperate, especially those who have been mandated for services against their will. Others cannot engage in goal setting because of age, developmental disabilities, or mental impairment. In these cases, the case manager may have to impose goals, drawing from options expected by the family, the agency in which he or she works, the courts, the community, and sometimes just plain common sense. Still, the worker should try to involve the client, regardless of the diagnosis or the severity of the problem, before imposing goals. The case manager should never assume that a client lacks the capacity to participate meaningfully in the process without first assessing the person.

Another more general role for the case manager in the goal-setting process is lending a positive vision and a sense of hope to clients and their families, no matter how difficult the situation or how slight the cooperation. While at times this may seem to be difficult or even impossible, it is always one of *your goals* with every client you see.

5. Developing and implementing a service intervention plan

By the time you have completed the first four steps in the case management process, the types of intervention you and the client will develop should be relatively clear. Following systems theory, you will direct intervention according to what you have learned from assessment. Case management interventions are often initially focused on the micro and mezzo levels. First, you will often do direct interventions, working with your client—crisis intervention, focused short-term casework, making referrals, advocacy for services, coordinating service delivery, or tracking service utilization and goal attainment. Secondly, you may be able to help the agency in which you work be more responsive to your clients. This might be done through training, reworking agency policies to make services more accessible, or involving clients as peer workers with new clients.

Third, you may work at the community intervention level to pave the way for support services for your clients, enhance existing resources at agencies, or develop resources where none exist. This type of intervention is often called community action, or community development. In many, if not most, cases, clients can be involved in this intervention process. Possible interventions at this level include: forming coalitions between agencies to coordinate services; forming and/or working with community groups around issues important to clients; engaging in voter registration drives; participating in programs that publicize community problems; and supporting fund-raising efforts for relevant causes. Interventions at this level do not have to be seen as controversial or "hell-raising." They are simply planned social work interventions at a community level, carried out with clear and focused goals in cooperation with fellow professionals and members of a community.

6. Evaluation

One of the most overlooked aspects of case management is evaluation. It is clear at this juncture of the social work profession and America's social problems that the very act of service delivery is not a sufficient indicator of success in the worker-client relationship or in the eyes of the community. We need to do more than show that we delivered case management services; how well did this joint process work? Fortunately, there is a way to answer this question. Technically, it is called determining goal attainment.

In determining the degree of goal attainment, the case manager asks questions like these: Was the drug problem alleviated and is the client in a drug treatment program? Did the client find a mental health center for his parent-child problem, and are he and his son going consistently? Is the abused child now stabilized and is her mother attending therapy sessions? Has housing been found and has the client moved in? Is money for a family's food now available and is it being used to improve nutrition? Has the client found a job and stayed in it?

Evaluation of this sort raises several issues. The first is the clarity of goals. Goals dictate the evaluation questions, and the more behaviorally specific the better. For example, if the goal is to decrease drug abuse and attend outpatient drug treatment, the simplest answer could be a simple "yes" to both parts of the first question. However, this is not as specific as a goal stating that drug abuse should decrease from daily usage to zero, with attendance at an outpatient treatment program three times a week for six months. With this kind of specificity, the case manager can estimate the client's drug use and the level of participation in treatment.

A second issue is the fact that some goals do not easily lend themselves to evaluation—for instance, an increase in self-esteem, an improved relationship with a child, greater cooperation between partners, or an improvement in an economic or housing situation. All of these are certainly worthwhile goals, but they do not lend themselves to easy evaluation.

Another issue raised in the evaluation process is how well client outcomes reflect on the case manager (Ryan & Sherman, 1994). If clients consistently fail to attain their goals, does it necessarily mean that the case manager is not doing a good job? Absolutely not! Client outcomes from case management are not the only factors to be considered. Some client problems are very resistant to measurable change and thus show little or no goal attainment in the short term. Examples include cocaine addiction, such developmental disorders as autism, and severe physical disabilities, such as a stroke or injuries from an accident. In many situations, too, there are simply not enough services to support reasonable goal attainment. In depressed areas, for example, jobs may be practically nonexistent, so that employment goals cannot be reached. Similar outcomes result when housing is not available for the homeless or when the waiting list for drug treatment is months long. Given the increasing breakdown of the social service and economic safety net in this country, there may be a consistent lack of goal attainment for a client group.

Another reason why clients may fail to meet case management goals is that caseloads are too large. Although each case management program sets a manager-client ratio, little research has been done to indicate what this ratio should be for a given client group or agency. In some programs, ratios are as low as 1:2, and in others the ratios may be as high as 1:500. While the judgment as to optimal staff-client ratios is based on many factors, there is always a critical mass where it becomes very difficult for case managers and clients to connect sufficiently to establish and track goals.

7. Termination

Appropriate termination should include one or more of the following criteria: clients have reached their goals; clients have satisfactorily demonstrated that they can self-manage their own movement towards goals; clients are successfully working with social service agencies, community support systems, or other referral sources. Remember that in case management it is not always your job to aid clients in reaching their long-term goals; rather you are the agent that helps them develop the community resources that can give them the support they need for the long haul. Therefore, a successful client termination from a case management program does not always mean that he or she has reached final goals. It should mean, however, that the client is on the road to goal attainment through some combination of personal and community resources.

There are, of course, situations where clients have reached their goals and need no further contact with you or any other community resource. Perhaps the client found a good job, obtained needed entitlements, or located decent housing. In other situations, when some or even all of the goals are unmet, other agencies or community support systems have taken over and are working with the client. This indicates that the goals of case management have been completely met, since you are no longer needed. The ultimate case management goal is to teach clients to be able to successfully identify, assess, and solve their problems using their own abilities. Appropriate termination from a case management program can certainly occur absent this outcome, but it is a goal for which case managers should strive.

People terminate social services, including case management, for many reasons, some of which have nothing to do with their goal attainment. Some leave because there is a time limit on the service, such as in managed care. Others terminate prematurely, which really means that they stop seeking our services before someone thinks they should. A goodly number of those who are not mandated to attend a program simply disappear. Regardless of why clients terminate, there are always two issues that should be addressed if possible during the termination process. The first one has to do with the service—assessing goal attainment, intervention strategies, "self-case management," and plans for the future. The second involves the relationship between the case manager and the client. The most important initial goal of termination from the case management process is that clients have a clear plan for the future. If they have reached all their goals, they should have plans for finding resources and solving problems on their own. If there is further work to be done, plans need to be clarified and reiterated. It should be made clear which agency and community organizations are supposed to remain involved in the client's continued support. Each such referral source should be contacted to assure a smooth transition from your case management activities to their service delivery system.

When clients terminate without much goal attainment and their cases are transferred to other agencies, it is not necessarily an indication that a case management system has failed. It may be an acknowledgement that the client needs a more focused and intensive service. But if many cases end this way, it is a good idea to evaluate such case management issues as intake, the availability of adequate community resources, and staff training.

Since case managers and clients develop relationships, some good and some not so good, there is also another dimension that should be addressed during termination. This is often called "closure." Whatever the nature of the relationship, it is usually helpful to review what happened between the parties—what was helpful and what was not. This process can be a good learning experience for both you and your client. Case managers need feedback from consumers, and clients need to evaluate the work they did and how their ability to form relationships helped or hindered their goal attainment. Often worker and client can share "warm fuzzies," which can feel good. Even when the relationship has not been pleasant, acknowledging this fact can be constructive if communicated without blame. When all is said and done, most people feel better when they have had the opportunity to say goodbye.

8. Follow-up

The most neglected part of the case management process is the follow-up phase, even though it requires the least amount of skill. All it requires is contacting the client or an agency professional at some future time to see how things have been going. This is usually done by phone or letter; rocket science technology is not required. A follow-up contact allows you to assess whether former clients need more support and how well they have been using community resources. Follow-up can also give you invaluable information in judging the appropriateness of your referrals, the effectiveness of referral agencies, and the role of the case management system you are part of in preparing clients for termination (Frankel & LaPorte, 1998; LaPorte & Frankel, 2000). You might find out, for example, that some agencies do not support clients for the long term as well as others.

Follow-up is valuable, but not all case managers do it. Why not? The answer is that it takes time and funding. Granted, a single phone call is not time consuming, but it may take many calls to track down former clients. With heavy caseloads in more and more agencies, workers often view the task of following up terminated clients as taking away valuable services from current clients. But evaluating the impact of case management services on clients after termination remains very important, especially in managed care programs (Marcendo & Smith, 1992).

For the Teacher or Trainer
Optional Exercises for Chapter 2
1. Systems theory

Divide students into groups of four to eight and then ask each group to divide into two teams. To each group, present a different social issue, such as a mother on welfare, an alcoholic in a family, a teen using drugs, a minority person who is arrested for petty theft, a single teenage girl who becomes pregnant, a male teenager who is expelled from school for violent behavior, or a college student who is flunking out. You may wish to embellish the circumstances of the issues. Ask one team to advocate for the person's personal responsibility for their actions and the other team to advocate for all of the family and societal reasons the person is behaving as they do. Let this discussion go on for ten to fifteen minutes, or longer if necessary. Then ask each group to report the major issues that came up. During the class discussion, focus on how these polar positions are integrated into a systems approach and the implications to case managers in working with clients. One question you may want to raise in this discussion is, What are the ethical and cultural implications of viewing social behavior solely as each person's personal responsibility?

2. *Current events and systems theory*
   Ask each student to cut out a newspaper article of interest to him or her. Then ask each to suggest, either in small group discussion, class discussion, or in an individual presentation to the class, how the social, economic, or political issue his or her article discusses can be viewed from a micro, mezzo, or macro level.

3. *Personal issues, systems theory, and problem solving*
   Ask each student to think of a current or past problem in his or her life or in the life of a family member. Then ask students to make three columns with the headings *micro, mezzo,* and *macro.* Have them fill in under each heading the personal, family, community, organizational, and policy issues that affect their chosen problems. Next ask them to think about and write down their, or their families', problem-solving methods, describing how problems are identified; how problems are assessed as to why they occur; how plans are made to ameliorate problems; how these plans are implemented, monitored, and evaluated; and how they or their families handle success or failure. Ask students to discuss what they wrote, either in a class discussion or in small groups. Consider participating in this exercise yourself and presenting to the class in order to model the exercise.

3   The Roles of a
Case Manager

During the process of case management with your clients, from the very inception of intake to the last follow-up contact, you will be taking on a number of helping roles. They will be played out in the three major domains of assessment and intervention of the helping process—direct intervention with clients, organizational/community interventions, and in the broader political/cultural/societal context. Each role requires you to focus on different problem-solving strategies, different skills, and different conceptual bases. Which roles you integrate into your own case management practice will depend on a number of factors, including time, your level of practice and conceptual experience, the nature of your clientele, and the agency where you work.

Direct Personal Support

No matter what other roles you play in the life of your clients, one of the foundations to helping is having a good supportive relationship with clients and offering them a sense of hope. The reasons for developing good rapport with clients in case management are somewhat different from those in other helping relationships.

Many casework theories discuss a good worker-client relationship as a necessary part of the curative process. This is generally true in traditional casework; if such a relationship does not develop over time, the client should probably be transferred to another worker. But this is not necessarily true in case management. In many situations, it is not possible to develop the kinds of relationships that would allow you to offer direct support, or allow it to be received. Some people who enter case management systems have been "burned" by social services or governmental agencies before coming to you. Their anger will not allow them to believe that their experience with you will be any different from the frustrating ones they have already had. Other clients are not able to connect because of mental or physical impairments. It may be difficult for you to engage meaningfully with autistic children, schizophrenics, or Alzheimer's patients. Or you may have a good relationship with a family member who has little power to resolve a problem, such as a young abused child or a frail old person. Finally, many clients who are forced to see you come figuratively kicking and screaming; they are uncommunicative at best and hostile at worst.

In all of these situations where good case management client-worker relationships are not possible, you can still be helpful. The bad news is that you will have to struggle to get good assessment information, and work harder to motivate clients to accept support. The good news is that by the very nature of the case management process, you are not alone in trying to connect with these people or in finding ways to help them. Your job is to activate a community resource network that will meet your clients' needs. Thus there are many agencies, professionals, community organizations, and individuals who will care about your clients, and, it is hoped, connect with them when you cannot.

Of course, having a good, trusting relationship with clients is desirable if it can be achieved. When someone comes to a case manager for help, the process is more pleasant if he or she likes the worker. This is as true for the helper as for the "helpee." You will enjoy your work much more when you have good relationships with your clients.

Good relationships have other positive side effects as well. People under stress need reassurance and a sense of hope. They do not normally allow case managers to give them this kind of support unless they feel some degree of trust and caring. Also, assessment is greatly enriched if clients and the important people around them actively participate in the process. People tend to share more with those they trust and respect.

One way to develop good relationships with resistant clients is to improve your connecting skills: showing empathy, active listening, focusing, reframing, summarizing, goal setting, negotiating, contracting, partializing, offering "warm fuzzies," and being able to accept anger and corrective feedback. All of these skills, and more, are part of case management training.

Crisis Intervention

As the name implies, crisis intervention is a limited and very focused strategy. Case managers do not normally offer casework or groupwork services to their clients, instead referring them to other agencies. But when case managers become aware of a crisis in their clients' lives, time can be a critical factor. If a crisis threatens to devastate a client before an appropriate referral can be found, it is the case manager's job to step in quickly to ameliorate the situation.

A crisis is defined by either the client, people around the client, a professional, or someone in the community. In general, when a crisis is perceived, the first responsibility of the case manager is to assess the severity of the situation. Crises might include a clear suicide gesture, the loss of welfare benefits, hospitalization for a serious illness or injury, a drug overdose, or a sudden death in the family. In many situations, however, it is not clear how serious the crisis is or whether it even is a crisis. One of the best examples of ambiguity is in the area of suicide or suicidal ideation (when a client talks or thinks about committing suicide). Experience and research have suggested that some suicide ideations are more serious than others. You may be facing a crisis when a client has a history of suicide attempts; has a clear plan of how she or he will carry out the suicide; is planning on a violent means of death; has put his or her affairs in order; or seems to be saying goodbye to you and others. Criteria like these appear on checklists developed by agencies specializing in crisis intervention, such as suicide hotlines.

It is not only the seriousness of a potential crisis that you have to assess, but also the time available to deal with it. In some cases you have no time at all; in others, you may be able to explore support options. It often depends on how clients and their families seem to be coping. For example, when a low-income employee loses his job, it is definitely a crisis, but if he is coping with the loss reasonably well and has support from savings, severance pay, or another working family member, you probably have time to explore options. But if the economic picture is grim and your client is on the verge of a nervous breakdown or about to revert to an addiction, you need to intervene immediately.

Obviously, good assessment skills are essential in determining how a worker should proceed in a potential crisis situation. From a case management perspective, crisis intervention can be as minimal as insuring that a referral source knows about the crisis and is dealing with it appropriately, to a full-fledged intervention, with the case manager acting as the central worker. In all cases, it is the case manager's responsibility to insure that the client gets the support needed to bring the situation under control.

When a case manager does act as the central person in crisis resolution, a number of skills are needed. First, as we have already said, the case manager must be able to quickly assess both the severity of a potential crisis and the time available for resolving it. This assessment, developed with the worker's empathy and support, should lead to an immediate set of goals with clear behavioral steps designed to reach them. These should incorporate tasks for both the client (if possible) and the case manager. The case manager also needs to enlist cooperative people in the client's natural and professional environment to help resolve the crisis. A case manager then needs to maintain frequent contact with the client and those enlisted until the immediate crisis has passed.

A case manager involved in crisis resolution needs to develop a clear plan so that the client can receive appropriate professional and family support over the longer term (the case management process being normally limited in time). This is not to say that the case manager needs to disappear. It does mean that the responsibility for long-term support should be transferred to other professionals and agencies. In a such a case, the worker should stay in touch with the client to make sure that long-term support is forthcoming; if it is not, the manager needs to locate other resources.

Crisis intervention is a fairly common role in case management, so regardless of the agency in which you practice, it is a good idea to learn more about managing crises. These will arise particularly in cases of drug and alcohol abuse, mental illness, domestic violence, death and bereavement, homelessness, and entitlement issues.

Short-Term Treatment Interventions

There will be many times when your assessment indicates that the problems presented to you as a case manager could be resolved in the short term. Short-term treatment is usually defined as methodologies that help people deal with a problem in one to twelve sessions. This approach has become popular in the current era of managed care, when mental-health costs are being scrutinized as never before. Short-term intervention can be successful in a number of areas, among them mental health, family problems, prevention education that focuses on health or mental health, budgeting, educational tutoring, and employment.

Short-term treatment requires that case managers be trained in relevant theoretical and practical foundations. Numerous theories lend themselves to brief intervention strategies—task-centered and solution-focused treatment, the behavioral approach, ego psychology, and cognitive interventions. All of these theoretical orientations have several things in common. First, a worker helps clients frame problems in ways that are manageable, dividing big problems into potentially solvable smaller ones. For example, a mother who is extremely distressed by her unmanageable adolescent son needs to focus on the specific behaviors that are troubling her. A couple with marital problems need to understand the particular issues that are causing conflict. A depressed man needs to focus on what is happening now in his life that is causing his unhappiness.

The second common factor in all brief interventions is the necessity of helping clients clarify what they can do in the short term, and what they should expect to be doing after treatment is completed. In other words, they need to translate their desires into clear, achievable goals and behavioral objectives. For example, a mother with a seemingly uncontrollable adolescent may set as a goal that he be "good" by the end of treatment. In this case specific goals could require that at the end of twelve weeks, the teenager will be coming in at night by curfew five out of five school nights and doing one household chore a day. An estranged couple will probably want to "get along better." What they specify at the end of brief treatment could be working out a monthly budget, negotiating a division of labor for child rearing, and going out on a "date" at least once a week. When a client says he wants to be less depressed at the end of treatment, goals could be framed as follows: Within eight weeks he will be getting out of the house at least five days a week—including attending day treatment three days a week and seeking a job two days a week—and taking his antidepressant medication every day.

The third factor that characterizes all brief therapies is that interventions are very specific from session to session. There are usually explicit "homework" assignments for clients. They are encouraged to be active participants in developing weekly interventions, although the worker often has to take an active and directive lead. In addition, there is a focus on weekly accountability and on making quick changes if something is not working.

Many of the problems and goals treated in the short term may seem superficial as compared with those fully achieved by long-term interventions, but time is a luxury rarely available in case management. If you judge that long-term treatment is indicated, you should refer clients to professionals and agencies that specialize in it.

Broker/Facilitator

After the assessment process, one of the most common case management tasks is to facilitate the helping process through linkages to social service agencies, governmental or voluntary community organizations, and other concerned people. This is most often done by making referrals. On the surface, this might seem to be a simple, almost rote process. Nothing could be further from the truth. Making a good referral assumes that case managers know the referral source and that there is a good fit between client needs and what is available. A case manager makes a referral not just to someplace that is supposed to take care of a problem, but to a place where it is highly probable that client needs will be met. Referring clients to sources that do not meet their needs increases people's frustration and lack of faith in their community support system. Poor and inappropriate referrals do nothing for your reputation as a case manager, either.

The only way case managers can really know whether a referral can help their clients is to know how an organization functions, its program components, the kinds of clients it serves, its track record, its staff, and how user-friendly it is.

One of the best ways to investigate a referral is to visit the site, talking with the professionals there, reading the organization's brochures and other published information, observing client flow, and asking about outcomes. Because you need to conduct your assessment in an open and professional way, you should make appointments and identify yourself, your employer, and your purpose. You need to educate yourself about the agency's work, the types of clients it serves, and how it would deal with referrals from your agency. Find out, specifically, how referrals should be made; what client eligibility requirements are; whom you need to communicate with; and who would be the referral's contact person in your own case management system. Other important issues center on finance: Are clients financed through public funds, such as Medicaid or other welfare benefits? Is there a sliding scale for fees? What is a client's personal responsibility for payments?

Having an open line of communication between the case manager and key referral staff is essential for the continued effectiveness of a referral source. It is helpful to have good professional relationships, and it never hurts to have friends in agencies as well. What you want to avoid if at all possible is strained relations between case management staff and agency referral sources. If such strains occur and persist, it is only your clients who will be hurt. So, when such situations happen—and they are bound to every once in a while— it is incumbent on case management staff to assess the problems and work to resolve them satisfactorily.

Another way to evaluate the effectiveness of referral sites is to ask clients about their experiences there. Tracking "client careers" through what is often an organizational conundrum is an excellent way to assess referral sources over time. This tracking is usually not a problem while clients are still part of your case management program. But after they terminate case management and are still using referrals, periodic follow-ups are needed to determine how agencies, organizations, and other community supports are performing. This process might involve periodic client- or consumer-satisfaction surveys.

Referral sources, like people, change over time. Staff members come and go; funding sources dry up and new ones are found; directors change policies. These changes can have profound effects on service delivery and will affect a referral agency's ability to meet the needs of its clients. Nothing is more annoying than to find out, sometimes months later, that one of your favorite referral sources has not been providing the services you expected. Keeping in touch with referral contacts will allow a case manager to track how changes within agencies affect clients.

Keeping track of political winds and governmental policies is very important in preparing clients for referrals to governmental agencies, such as social security. Having good contacts in these agencies, along with following the political process on TV and in the newspapers, will help you know what changes are being considered even before they show up in regulations. Advanced knowledge can help you begin exploring referral alternatives, especially when entitlements are being curtailed or cut.

Clearly, the case manager's role of facilitator in referring clients for services is much more complicated than it might seem on the surface. It requires competency in organizational assessment, professional communication, tracking, and program evaluation. These are skills that can be learned and enhanced through training and experience.

Along with referral, facilitation in case management may involve enhancing the support opportunities in a client's family or friendship systems, or connecting clients with new people-to-people helping networks in the community. The activation and empowering of families, friends, religious or ethnic affiliations, and neighborhood centers around a client may turn out to be the most important factor in the long-term success of case management activities. While it may not always be possible to link and involve informal supports, their potential should always be explored. Often when you work with vulnerable populations—children, the aged, and those who are impaired mentally, emotionally, developmentally, or physically—you will need to consider their family members as clients, along with the "identified patient." They are the center of a natural community support system, and their stability, motivation, and ability to help each other need to be assessed and made part of the helping process to the extent possible. You may find that much of your time as a case manager is spent working to motivate and empower this naturally occurring support system.

Enabler/Teacher/Mediator

The goal of case management in many instances is to have clients take increasing levels of responsibility for achieving identified and agreed-upon goals. The role is described as enabling. Your ability to increase a client's self-confidence is a critical part of this incremental process. As a case manager you must be aware of each client's capacity to engage in the process and be able to encourage increasing levels of responsibility. Moving from doing *for,* to doing *with,* to having clients do *for themselves,* increases client self-confidence, self-sufficiency, and independence. Gauging when clients are ready and able to do *for themselves* requires an accurate and continuing sense of where the client is in the helping process. Enabling a client to take acceptable and increasing levels of risk is one criterion that can be used in assessing effectiveness in case management.

At times you will be called upon to act as a teacher, providing learning opportunities for clients. Activities commonly presented in case management programs include information about community resources, mental illness, health, sexually transmitted diseases (STD's), and alcohol and drugs. You may find opportunities to use group discussion and role play to help clients practice behaviors that will help them manipulate service bureaucracies.

The case manager will at times have to assume the role of mediator in disputes between clients, between clients and community services, or between personnel in agencies who are involved with your clients. There is a significant difference between a mediator role and an advocate role. The advocate is clearly taking one side; the mediator is trying to remain neutral and not favor one side or the other. Obviously, this can be tricky. In mediation, the case manager tries to bring the parties involved to a common ground or understanding of the conflict, recognizing the legitimate interests of each party. The goal in these cases is, of course, for the case manager to mediate a reasonable resolution of the conflict. Even when this goal cannot be reached, a good mediator still attempts to be perceived as neutral, so as to be available to mediate another day.

Advocate

Client advocacy is one of the most important case management roles. In fact, one could make a case for regarding other roles as subsidiary to that of advocate. Advocacy means that a case manager acts on behalf of clients who are unable or unwilling to act on their own behalf. Actually, advocacy may occur when clients are able to act on their own, but when it is judged that a case manager could intervene more effectively. This is apt to happen with clients who lack capacity for one reason or another—such as with children, retarded citizens, the elderly, or those who are emotionally or physically impaired. Addicted or suicidal patients may fall into this category as well. Some clients are simply unwilling to act on their own behalf, often those who are mandated for treatment or those who live in inpatient settings.

Client advocacy can also be helpful when it is clear that case managers have more power or professional connections than their clients. There are times when it is essential to "grease the wheels" to find services, especially when prior experience has shown that clients have little power to influence a social service or health system. For instance, if a client is turned away from an agency or governmental entitlement and you believe that eligibility requirements have been met, it is time to use your professional muscle to do what the client couldn't. Sometimes you may have a formal or informal connection with an agency that can be used on your client's behalf.

Advocacy is a good way to show clients that you care and are on their side. In such cases, advocacy intervention is resorted to even if the clients could have acted on their own.

Case managers advocate for their clients in many ways, of which making referrals or appointments is one of the most obvious. Advocacy also includes seeking out and assessing the effectiveness of community resources; making it possible for clients to gather information and facilitate program access; communicating directly with relevant professionals and/or family members about client welfare and needs; and acting as a mediator to resolve conflicts between a client and agency. Other kinds of case manager support could also qualify as advocacy: shopping or cooking for a client, for example, or babysitting a client's children when no one else is available.

It is often unclear how much and to what degree case managers should be involved in client advocacy. Whenever case managers act on behalf of their clients, even just to make a referral, they are acting as client substitutes. Every time this happens, and often it must, clients are losing the opportunity to practice advocating for themselves. By definition, practicing any new behavior, including assertive skills, community assessment, and self-advocacy, is a learning process that includes making mistakes (Wehmeyer & Metzler, 1995). At times the wisdom of Solomon may be required in order to decide when to back off and support clients in their attempts to act for themselves, when to advocate for them, and when to find some kind of middle ground. We must constantly remember that the more clients learn to act for themselves and their families, the more independent and self-sufficient they will become. An additional value of self-advocacy is that people become more involved in their community and with people who share their life problems. Thus case managers should not take on the advocacy role as a habit without careful consideration.

Client advocacy can also be viewed at an organizational and community level (Gelman, 1989). When case managers work in their organizations to make services more effective and efficient, they are certainly advocating for all clients. Similarly, when workers get involved in community activities that highlight serious community problems or service deficits, when they initiate service development, when they organize people for political and social change—all of these actions are ultimately acts of client advocacy. Sometimes organizational and community advocacy is the most significant kind of intervention a case manager can be involved in, especially when resources are inadequate, inefficient, or nonexistent.

Client advocacy is an essential part of case management practice, and the more effectively case managers master the prerequisite skills, the better they can serve their clients. However, an interesting philosophical dilemma arises here. Assume for the moment that there are only a finite number of available resources in a community—say, 100 slots for outpatient drug treatment and 1,000 clients in various case management programs in desperate need of treatment. The addicted clients with more effective professional advocates will have a better chance of getting one of the 100 available slots than the others. Perhaps those case managers had better contacts in the drug program, or they may just be more persuasive. In any case, what this dynamic sets up is a subtle competition among case managers to garner for their clients as much as possible of the inadequate resources available. By definition, successful client advocacy in the face of inadequate resources comes at a cost to less fortunate clients.

On one level, this success is just the result of good case management. On a larger scale, however, it raises the question: What are our professional responsibilities in a community when resources are inadequate and every client placement means that many others cannot get needed services? There are no simple answers to this important question. Professionals involved in case management need to take a broad community view of client populations and the services needed to support the disenfranchised, the poor, those who face discrimination, and others in need. Client advocacy at the organizational, community, and political level may be the most cogent response to resolving this dilemma.

Service Coordinator

Case managers often find themselves in a service coordination role. It can develop in several ways, either formally or informally, depending on how complicated the solutions for a client's case become. Many case management programs are designed to be the service coordinators for a fixed amount of time. For example, there are intensive case management programs, called ICM's, that work with their clients very closely for four to eight weeks. ICM's are common in forensic after-care; in working with the chronically mentally ill; when dealing with families to prevent children from being placed in foster care; and in addictions work. The assumption behind intensive case management starts with the idea that if clients can be immediately connected to a variety of community agencies—housing, welfare, treatment, medication, and so on—the initial presenting problems will be ameliorated. It is further assumed that once the ICM worker establishes and coordinates this community support system, clients will be maintained indefinitely at a stable level.

Case managers in ICM systems have their work cut out for them. They not only need a comprehensive grasp of available resources but also have to quickly coordinate these services by acting as the hub in a social service wheel. In addition, since ICM case managers have a limited time to act as service coordinators, they must quickly establish communication among clients, agencies, and professionals, one of whom will (hopefully) take over their role. As you can imagine, this is no easy task. When clients terminate from ICM systems, there may not be another central community coordinator to pick up the slack over the long haul. Thus the central problem facing ICM case managers is not only to support initial client stabilization, but also to build a community resource coalition with the client in as proactive a role as possible.

The service-coordinating role may develop informally as a set of services develops around a client. Professionals and agencies may begin looking to you as the central resource person for clients simply because you have spent so much time trying to coordinate services on their behalf. You may find that other professionals are calling you to report problems even though you are no longer officially on the case. Social service coordinating functions in your community may be lacking, and you are seen as the only show in town. If you cannot continue in this role indefinitely, you will need to address this problem with staff in your agency and those in other community organizations. Clearly, there are clients who need long-term case management support. If it is not forthcoming, they may become recidivists, which is just a technical term for clients who end up needing the same types of services over and over again.

The Tracking/Follow-Up Role

One of the most neglected roles in case management is the follow-up role. Follow-up requires not only the time to track clients after case management termination, but also the organizational will to expend the effort. To find clients six or twelve months after they have left your agency can be a daunting task, particularly in programs that deal with transient populations. Even with people who are not so transient, they change jobs, residences, or phone numbers as part of normal life.

However difficult, tracking former clients is valuable. First, for people with whom you made a personal connection, it is good to know how they are doing. But beyond satisfying personal needs, learning the long-term status of clients is an indication of how well your case management program is doing and how well other professional and community support systems are performing, too.

Imagine for a moment if you will that you are part of an incredibly effective case management program, connecting clients to services and community resources that quickly resolve their presenting problems. What if you found out that after six months, most of your clients were reporting the same problems that brought them to you in the first place? What would this say about the true effectiveness of the case management program? What would this say about the community's ability to provide long-term support to individuals and families?

It is only through long-term follow-up, which is another form of evaluation (an outcome measure), that case managers find out whether their solutions to client problems are helpful over time. When other agencies are supposed to pick up the slack for client maintenance but do not, it will have profound implications for a case management program. At the very least, clients may have to be better empowered to independently support themselves before termination. Long-term follow-up also allows you to assess the quality of referral sources; if treatment plans arranged with other agencies are not being continued over time, there is a problem.

You and your agency do not necessarily have to take responsibility for the failure of other community and governmental support systems. Some of these failures are systemic, occurring when welfare laws change or the American economy deteriorates. Obviously, government policies, especially fiscal cutbacks, affect the ability of the mentally ill, the homeless, and the elderly—to name just a few—to maintain themselves with dignity. Case management programs cannot be held accountable for these assaults on the social service, economic, and health care safety net. However, without knowing specifically what has happened to former clients, it is very difficult to know how to focus your case management program, your community action plans, and your efforts to design better long-term community support systems for people in need.

Follow-up in case management takes time, energy, and money. This role for case managers is becoming more prevalent as professionals and funders understand its importance. Yet it is easy to see why administrators often have to make hard decisions concerning case manager time allocations in the face of ballooning caseloads and decreasing budgets. This does not make the issue any less important; it just means that case managers may have to be more creative and insistent in tracking former clients.

For the Teacher or Trainer
Optional Exercises for Chapter 3
1. Comfort with case manager roles

Ask students to list the seven case manager roles discussed in this chapter. For each role, ask them to indicate on a 3-point scale their present comfort level, with 3 being "great comfort," 1 being "some discomfort," and 2 being "in the middle." Collect these sheets, put the seven roles on the board, and list the students' scores for each role. Using these collected scores, discuss the overall results as well as why people might have reported less or more comfort with specific roles.

2. *Special issues related to case manager roles*
In a class discussion, present an ethical, cultural, racial, or religious issue that interacts with a case manager role. For instance:

What ethical issues arise in tracking a client over time after termination?

What are the issues involved in teaching about STD's or pregnancy prevention?

What are the issues involved in intervening in a crisis when someone does not want your help, for example, suicide prevention or drug treatment?

What are the implications of a short-term treatment mandated by an insurance company when the problem can only be solved in a long-term treatment?

What are the ethical and practical issues involved in advocating for a client when doing so might put the case manager's job at risk, for example, when a client has real problem with the agency administration or when the case manager suspects his or her supervisor of inappropriate behavior toward a client?

What are the issues that arise when advocating for a pregnant teen whose parents don't want her to have an abortion?

4 An Example of Case Management

At this juncture, it should prove helpful to review a single case to see how case management works. We will go through the eight steps of the case management process and view the case through the lenses of three levels for assessment and intervention over an eight-week period.

Bill, an eight-year-old, is referred to a case manager because he has been abused by his mother. Bill's teacher reported the situation to the state protective services division when she saw unexplained bruises on Bill's arms. The case manager is employed by a state division of children's services. Mom is unemployed, without a high school education. She receives welfare benefits, and lives in a small apartment she shares with a man whom she calls her boyfriend. Mom was never married, and Bill's father has shown no interest in him since he was born.

Defining the Problem
Clearly, the fact that Bill is being hit and bruised is the central problem in this situation. However, as we get further into the assessment process, we will be adding other problems. As you will see, good assessment cycles through Steps 1, 2, and 3, a number of times before we go on to Step 4.

Determining the Severity of the Problem
The presenting problem is very severe, and thus needs immediate attention.

Developing Hypotheses Concerning Why the Problem Is Occurring

Understanding *why* this abuse is occurring is a critically important and complex task. The answers to this question do not in any way excuse or condone the abuse, but understanding its causes should lead to an intervention strategy that will allow this mother and son to function successfully as a family. At the *micro level,* personal/interpersonal, we can look at the dynamics between mother and son, and the psychological makeup of each of them. Is Mom the one who is abusing the child, or is it the boyfriend? Does Mom want to keep the boy? Is she physically, mentally, and emotionally able to parent a child? Is she also being abused by her boyfriend? Are drugs or alcohol a problem for the mother and/or the boyfriend? What is Mom's present mental and physical state of health? How easy is Bill to take care of? What special problems does he bring to the situation, physically, mentally, or emotionally? Beyond the two of them, what interpersonal supports do they have? Where is the father, and what role, if any, do relatives play in their lives? Does Bill have any friends? Does his mother have friends or other people she can rely on?

The *mezzo level,* the institutional category, guides assessment into the practical issues that could cause stress in this family and create an atmosphere conducive to child abuse. For example (as we know from our own lives), economic factors can create major tension. What is Bill's mother's educational level and does she have job skills? Does she have enough money to live on? Is there sufficient food, heat, clothing? Is their living situation acceptable? Can Mom work? Is she able to get to work? Do relatives or the boyfriend contribute anything to help out? What is the mother's connection to religious and community groups? What use has she made of agencies that offer financial, educational, medical, and emotional and parental supports in her community? Are quality child-care programs available and accessible? Is the school Bill attends supportive of him and his mother?

The *macro level,* involving policy/political issues, guides case managers into a number of areas. What are the governmental programs and policies that seem to contribute to this family's problem? For example, if the family is poor, what are the rules governing how much money the mother is entitled to? Is the local government trying to gain child support from the absent father? Are there programs, public or private, that offer job training and other educational opportunities for single moms? If child care is available, is it accessible to women like Bill's mother? Do the school system's policies deal fairly and openly with her? Do policy and rules make it possible for her (and other parents) to access services and entitlements?

Another macro level issue is how this family's racial, ethnic, and/or gender identity affect both mother and child, not only personally, but in their ability to gain access to services that could reduce their stress. If there is discrimination, we know that its effects are profound.

It should be clear to you by now that developing hypotheses about causes is a complex and comprehensive process. You will gain confidence as you gain experience, and most agencies offer a good deal of systematic support through various assessment instruments. Many of you will find that the agency in which you work will ask you to focus your assessment on specific areas, based on agency or community norms, the demands of funding sources, or limitations caused by time or workload. As a professional case manager, however, you should know how the systems approach guides assessment so that you will be able to make your own judgments about how much assessment information you need in order to understand the problems you deal with.

As you collect assessment information, you will be formulating a hypothesis as to what is causing the problem. In the case of Bill and his mother, it should be evident that there is no single cause of the abuse; rather, there is a cluster of causal factors at each of the three levels that is unique to this particular family. True, there are some common factors among families that seem to be correlated with child abuse, such as stress, drug and alcohol abuse, and a parent's history of childhood abuse. But each case presents a unique assessment puzzle. A good assessment should always lead the case manager to develop intervention strategies at two or three system levels. Our assumption is that since client problems are being affected at all three levels, interventions need to involve as broad an approach as possible.

In the case of Bill and his mother, the case manager found that Mom had a problem with alcohol. She also had a very low tolerance for Bill's acting-out behavior and seemed to lack basic parenting skills. She expressed dissatisfaction with her live-in boyfriend but felt trapped with him because she couldn't survive financially alone. Mom had very few friends, could not identify any job skills or career goals, and appeared depressed.

The worker suspected, based on descriptions of Bill's classroom behavior, that he might have an Attention Deficit Disorder. It was unclear whether the teacher or the school were dealing with his acting-out in an effective way.

Establishing Goals

After two meetings, the case manager made some tentative hypotheses about causal factors in Bill's case. The very nature of developing hypotheses means that workers cannot know if they are correct unless they lead to successful interventions. Therefore this case manager used what was learned to suggest the following initial short- and long-term goals:

Micro level

1. Physical abuse directed at Bill must immediately cease.
2. Mom needs to decrease and then eliminate her consumption of alcohol.
3. Mom needs to learn effective positive parenting skills.
4. Mom needs to clarify her relationship with her live-in boyfriend.
5. Bill needs to be evaluated for possible ADD diagnosis.
6. Bill needs to make friends.

Mezzo level

1. Bill's school needs assessment to see whether the staff can control Bill's acting-out in class.
2. Mom needs a job.

3. Mom needs to find an after-school child-care program (a "latchkey" program).
4. Resources need checking to see whether Bill's father can be made to contribute to his support.
5. Mom needs more connections with community groups.

Macro level

1. There should be a more effective spectrum of services to support addicted mothers who abuse their children.

You will notice at this point that the definition of the problem as originally outlined in Step 1 has become much broader. We can now go back and add these problems to Step 1 and assess their severity in Step 2. The definition of the problem list and problem severity would now be:

Problem	Severity
1. Child abuse	High
2. Mom's alcohol addiction	High
3. Mom's poor parenting skills	Moderate
4. Bill's acting-out behavior at home	High
5. Bill's lack of friends	Moderate
6. Bill's inability to control his school behavior	Moderate
7. Mom's lack of money and a job	High
8. Lack of after school child care for Bill	Moderate
9. Lack of Dad's involvement in Bill's life	Moderate
10. Relationship issues with live-in boyfriend	Moderate
11. Mom's disconnectedness with her community	Moderate
12. The lack of a comprehensive network for addicted parents who abuse their children	Moderate

We see that this worker's list is now considerably augmented since the initial phase of assessment. Good case management also assumes that the client—Mom and Bill in this case—were actively involved in developing this list and determining the level of severity, which would indicate the urgency and intensity of the work that needs to be done. We would also assume that Mom and Bill helped develop goals that will lead to a service plan.

Developing and Implementing a Service Intervention Plan

It is now time to develop a service plan, using the resources available in this family system and the community, or some that can be augmented or developed. With Mom and Bill's cooperation and involvement, the worker set out the following service plan.

Micro level

1. Bill is to be placed immediately in a short-term foster care facility, with frequent supervised visits from his mother.

2. Mom is to be referred to a comprehensive day treatment program for her alcohol problem, with the goal of decreasing and eventually eliminating her drinking.

3. Mom is to be referred to a weekly parent training/parent support group in order to improve her parenting skills.

4. Mom and her boyfriend are to attend short-term counseling.

5. Bill is to be referred for psychological testing to see if he has an ADD.

6. Bill is to be connected with after-school and weekend activities at the local YMCA.

Mezzo level

1. The school social worker will be told that Bill is being evaluated for ADD, and asked what programs the school system offers for this diagnosis.

2. Mom will be helped to identify and enroll in a job training program.

3. Mom will be given sufficient information so that she can apply for after-school child-care benefits while she is enrolled in job training.

4. Mom will be given the number of a legal aid attorney who will explore whether Bill's father can contribute child support.

5. Mom will be referred to a local church of her religious persuasion whose pastor is active in drug-addiction programs.

Macro level

1. The case manager registers Mom to vote.
2. The case manager joins a task force in order to form a coalition of community agencies to deal with child abuse.

Evaluation

To evaluate the success of the initial service plan after eight weeks and over a long-term period after termination (six months, for example), the case manager needed to track the effect of the referrals, the client's attendance, and the outcome of the intervention over time. If it was clear that the plan was not working, an alternative plan had to be developed. In this case, there were two basic ways of evaluating the success of the service plan: through the client's personal report, and through phone calls to agency staff where referrals were made (with the client's consent, of course). We should restate here that case managers need to respect client confidentiality; all community contacts should be explicitly cleared with clients unless there is a mandated professional relationship between the case management system and a particular agency. Even in those situations, it is important to let clients know how you will be following up the effectiveness of the service plan. At the eight-week mark, an evaluation of the case management service showed the following outcome:

Micro level

1. Bill was immediately placed in foster care. Mom visited him two evenings a week and spent all day Saturday with him.
2. Mom was enrolled in a day treatment program. Her attendance was over 90 percent at day treatment individual and group therapy sessions, and she attended 80 percent of her AA meetings. She also got an AA sponsor. She reported no alcohol consumption during this period.
3. Mom attended a weekly parent support group six out of eight possible times during this period. She reported that

she enjoyed the group and was learning more positive ways to deal with Bill.

4. Mom and her boyfriend completed three sessions with a counselor, who helped them clarify their relationship with each other and with Bill.

5. After a psychological evaluation, Bill was diagnosed with ADD. He is currently taking Ritalin under the supervision of a psychiatrist.

6. Bill has not yet been enrolled in the YMCA program. Both the foster mother and Bill's mom report that they have no transportation to get him there.

Mezzo level

1. It is not yet clear to what extent the school system can help Bill and other children with ADD. The school social worker reports that Bill's behavior in the classroom has improved.

2. Mom has enrolled in an electrician apprenticeship program, and has had excellent attendance. According to program staff, she is doing very well.

3. As part of the training program, Mom was able to receive an after-school child-care benefit. Since Bill is still in foster care, she has not yet needed to use it, but hopes that Bill will be allowed to come home.

4. Mom has visited the legal aid attorney twice to try to get child support from Bill's father. According to the attorney, this is in process.

5. Mom is attending church now on Sundays. She has joined its Parents Against Drugs committee, and has attended four of their meetings.

Macro level

1. Mom registered to vote.

2. The case manager attended three agency coalition meetings to improve community services for addicted parents who abuse their children.

As you can see, not all of the goals have been reached, and some lead to new goals such as more involvement from Bill's school, enrollment at the Y, and better child-care services.

Termination

At the end of eight weeks, the case manager presented these findings to the court, and Bill was allowed back home with Mom and her boyfriend. While the case manager would still be involved in terms of follow-up, it was clear that the responsibility for continued success would now be more in Mom's hands and those of the agencies with whom Mom and Bill were working.

The case manager arranged a meeting with Mom's workers from the alcohol treatment center and her job training site. Mom was included in this meeting. Everyone came to an agreement on the following plan.

1. Mom would continue to attend the alcohol day treatment program and her AA meetings.

2. Mom would continue to attend her parent support group. She would utilize their system for calling her "buddy" if she felt that she was about to abuse her child.

3. Bill would be enrolled in a weekly play group at the local mental health center for children with an ADD diagnosis. Mom would consult with their staff every week when she dropped him off there.

4. Mom would attend scheduled parent conferences with Bill's teacher.

5. Mom would continue her job training with the goal of getting a job at the end of the year's apprenticeship.

6. Mom would find a family child-care program in her neighborhood for Bill to attend after school.

7. Mom would continue to consult with the legal aid attorney about child support from Bill's father.

8. Mom would continue her church activities.

9. The case manager would make a home visit once every eight weeks for the next six months.

10. A worker from the day treatment program and one from the job training program would call the case manager once a month to report Mom's progress.

11. In six months there would be another case evaluation meeting with Mom, the case manager, and the day treatment and job training workers.

Notice that the termination plan dictated expected behavior not only for Mom, but also for the two community workers and the case manager. Everyone has a role in the next six months to help support Mom in reaching her goals, and to help Bill as well.

In addition to the team meeting that developed the termination plan, the case manager and Mom had an individual session together to further long-range goals and to say goodbye. This personal contact was important to them both as they had developed a close working relationship in the preceding weeks.

Follow-Up

The case manager's plans for follow-up were made clear during the termination process. There was to be phone contact from the two referral agencies, and at least two home visits before the end of the six-month follow-up team meeting. When this type of follow-up is planned, the case manager needs to have a "tickler" system to make sure that these contacts are made. In particular, since both community workers were supposed to initiate monthly phone calls, the case manager needs to see that they do so. Given that this case manager, like most, will continue to have many additional clients, it would be easy to lose track of terminated clients and their plans for follow-up.

For the Teacher or Trainer
Optional Exercises for Chapter 4
1. Confidentiality
On a blackboard, ask students to brainstorm a list of every type of person in their lives in the following domains: personal

and family, school, and work or intern setting. For example, in their personal and family life this could include friends, neighbors, wives/husbands/partners, children, parents, grandparents, other relatives, and so on. School life would yield fellow students in this class, fellow students in other classes, and teachers. Contacts in a work or intern setting might include colleagues, supervisors, administrators, clients, and other professionals. When the lists are completed, ask students to form groups of five to ten and choose a secretary. The secretary will list each type of person on a piece of paper—sister, boyfriend, colleague, and so on. Then he or she will ask the group for a show of hands if that person knows *anything* about their client cases, even if the client's name has not been mentioned. The secretary records the number of hands for each person on the list. After each group has finished the teacher asks for the tally and records it on the blackboard, adding up the totals after all of the groups have reported.

Compare what you see on the board with the ethical confidentiality standards from the social work, nursing, or psychological professions. Ask students whether they had clear contracts with clients to discuss anything about their cases with each of the people listed in their lives.

2. Problem specification

Pair students for a role play: one will be the client, the other the worker. The client will come up with at least three problems. The worker has to help the client define each one in a behaviorally specific way, with at least one example of a measurable behavioral indicator as part of the definition. Examples of problem areas might be aggression, depression, anxiety, low self-esteem, poor self-concept, low ego strengths, phobias, assertive problems, drug addiction, any DSM-IV-TR diagnosis, or antisocial behavior.

3. Determining severity

List any type of problem on the blackboard. Examples could include homelessness, suicide ideations, AIDS, or job loss. Divide students into small groups and have them develop a hypothetical five-point rating scale with a 5 meaning that the problem is very severe and must be dealt with immediately and a 1 meaning that the problem is not severe at this time. Have each group discuss their 5-point list with the larger group.

4. Developing assessment hypotheses

A. Present a case summarizing psycho-social information. List the three system levels—micro, mezzo, and macro—on the board. Lead a discussion about the possible reasons, at each level, why the client problem is occurring.

B. Have students write a short piece on a personal problem or one that has troubled a friend, family member, or relative. Ask them to assess at each of the three system levels why the problem has occurred. They can submit their analyses to you for feedback or share their assessments with the class.

5. Goal setting

A. Present a number of "decreasing" goals to the class, such as easing depression, stopping criminal behavior, decreasing drinking, or ceasing antisocial behavior. Ask students to define a hypothetical behavioral indicator as a baseline level and set a reasonable goal to be achieved in three months. Then ask them to develop at least one "increasing" goal for every decreasing goal to replace what the client won't be doing. They should be behaviorally specific for this goal as well.

B. Ask students to develop three-month goals for individuals dealing with one of these problems: being fired, losing welfare benefits, becoming homeless, suffering a heart attack, arrest for drug possession, a diagnosis of Alzheimer's.

C. Present students with vague goals and ask how they could be improved. Examples could be to improve ego strengths; improve self-esteem; see life in a more positive way; have a better attitude; behave better in class; be a better parent; improve vocational skills; find better housing; improve health.

6. Ethnic, cultural, and religious issues

Ask students to briefly review the case example in this chapter. Then ask them to form small groups and assign each group a different ethnic, cultural, or religious background, such as African American, Caucasian, Latino, religious Christian, religious Jewish, religious Muslim; homosexual, or bisexual. If you wish, the groups may be composed of people who are themselves members of the indicated background. Ask each group to review the case again, but this time focusing on the implications of their group's background for each step in the process. Allow twenty to thirty minutes for these small group discussions. Then, ask each group to summarize their discussion and involve the class in these discussions as well.

Part 2
Case Management Skills

5 Interpersonal, Connecting, and Information-Gathering Skills

We have discussed the case management process in terms of an eight-step sequence of events: problem specification; determining the severity of the problem; assessing causation; setting goals; intervention; evaluation; termination; and follow-up. In the context of this process, there are many skills you can learn or improve to make you more effective. Many of them are generic; they can be applied throughout the process. Some skills, on the other hand, may seem more applicable to certain steps than to others. It is difficult to predict which skills will be more useful at any particular time. Therefore, while we have divided skills into several categories, remember that any of them can be applied at almost any step in the case management process.

Establishing good relationships with clients and the relevant people in their lives is important in the case management process. From the time the case manager first makes contact with a client, the two need to establish rapport (Coffey, 2003). The interpersonal skills necessary to build rapport are obviously important at this stage. As relationships develop, many other skills will come into play. As we review them, you will notice that as you increase your competence in these skill areas, they will be useful not only in your professional life, but in your personal life as well.

First Impressions and Diversity Issues

When people meet, the first sense they make use of is the visual. Your client will notice, among other things, the decor and cleanliness of your office and the clothes you and other staff wear. The agency in which you work may or may not have rules governing how offices may be decorated or setting up a dress code. No matter. You need to be aware that your setting and how you look will affect a client's first impression of you before you even open your mouth.

You should also be aware that obvious and subtle differences in appearance between you and your clients *always* cue cultural, ethnic, religious, racial, political, age, and sexual issues. First encounters raise these issues because of the stereotypes and prejudices we grow up with, as well as our later experiences. Whether or not you attend to these issues depends on how obvious the differences appear to be, your sense of your client's feelings about the differences, and your awareness of your own feelings about diversity. For example: In American culture, a racial difference between client and case manager is an obvious issue that must be faced. The same holds true with ethnic diversity. When a Mexican American meets a Cuban American, an Asian American meets an East Indian American, or a Caucasian American meets an Arab American, each brings stereotypes to the encounter.

The United States may have been established on a foundation of religious and political freedom, but that doesn't mean that people are always comfortable with diversity. Imagine the possible issues raised when a Jewish worker meets a born-again Christian client, or a Muslim client faces a Hindu worker. In areas where political issues have polarized communities, people can be very sensitive to these differences. Similarly, every time a man meets a woman, role expectations and stereotypes abound. To make matters even more complex, issues of sexual orientation have to be considered—your own and your comfort level in working with clients who have a different orientation.

There is no way that you can form good working relationships with clients unless you are sensitive to diversity issues. The question is not whether diversity issues between you and your clients exist—they always do. The question you must address is whether a particular difference between you and a client is affecting the professional relationship to the point that it impairs your client's ability to attain his or her goals. There are no easy answers to this question, but you should raise it in your mind for every client. It could be the focus of supervision and training.

You should also consider discussing diversity issues with your clients when it seems appropriate.

How you use body and eye contact is also connected to diversity issues. For example, it is natural for most Americans to shake hands during introductions. But a man should never do so with an Orthodox Jewish or Muslim woman. Nor is it ever appropriate to touch an East Indian with your left hand. The quality and intensity of eye contact, too, has different meanings in various cultures.

Whatever the cultural differences, however, you should be able to connect with clients, especially in the initial sessions. The foundation of this skill is having a friendly look on your face and being able to make good eye contact. You may think you measure up well in this regard, but you might be surprised by people's initial perception of you. This is a matter worth checking out with your fellow case management trainees.

Basic Interviewing Skills

While good interviewing may be instinctive, there are many ways to make the process more effective. Your goal during the initial case management interview is, of course, to obtain necessary information from your clients, to get to know them as people, and to begin the process of building a good professional relationship. Many of the skills we discuss enhance these goals, but you should pay special attention to a few very basic ones.

First, you should have a good sense of the information you need to obtain from the initial interview. This will allow you to spend more time looking at your client and less time with your face buried in a form. Most people like to have their worker make eye contact with them, at least intermittently, during an interview.

Second, you need to be clear about how you will record the information you gather. Case managers often have forms to fill out during the interview process. If you are constantly writing with your head down during an interview, it will impair your ability to begin building a relationship, creating trust, and inspiring a sense of hope. Some case managers learn to write quickly as clients talk; others write in short spurts after receiving information, interspersing eye contact with writing; still others talk to clients for awhile and then write for awhile. It is also possible to remember whole sessions, or parts of them, and fill out forms after clients have left. Practicing process recording helps with this skill. In general, most case managers need to practice getting information and filling out forms during an interview while staying in good contact with their new clients.

A third basic interviewing skill is the art of asking questions. Without training, most people develop a style of interview question-asking behavior. More often than not, an hour of asking questions develops into a rhythmic singsong melody, interesting at first but boring after awhile. Clearly, case managers have to gather a lot of information in initial interviews. However, they can intersperse questions with statements and comments about what the client is saying. Even the act of asking a question can be done in different ways. For example, you can ask *closed-ended* questions or *open-ended* questions. A closed-ended question would be, "How many children do you have?" The answer requires only a number. Or to the question "Do you use condoms?" a simple yes or no is the response. The same questions could be asked in an open-ended way: "What can you tell me about your children?" Or "How do you protect yourself during sex?" When using closed-ended questions, you tend to get very specific information, which at times is exactly what you want. Open-ended questions tend to give you more information, but are not as focused. There is nothing wrong with asking questions either way during an interview, but it helps not to rely too much on one style.

Another way to vary the information-gathering process is to use statements instead of questions. Instead of asking, "What do you and your child fight about?" you could say, "I would be interested in knowing what you and your child fight about." You obtain the same information, but with a statement instead of a question. Instead of asking, "How do you get along with your parents?" you could state, "Tell me about your relationship with your parents." Alternating open-ended questions, closed-ended questions, and statements in the interview process will help you stay in better contact with your clients. (You will find, however, that closed-ended questions and statements often need the additional skill of *furthering*, while open-ended questions and statements often need *focusing* skills; we will cover these skills shortly.)

Attending to Personal Issues and Commonalities

When clients and workers make first contact in the case management process, both usually expect that there is business to be conducted; it is not meant to be a social contact, as when two people meet with the potential of a friendship between them. Yet whenever people encounter each other in whatever circumstances, curiosity about the other is natural and there is often a need to have some small part of the friendship dynamic in the relationship. The relationship between professional case manager and the client is no different. You can help put your clients at ease if you act in a naturally friendly way as you get to know them. You can do this in a number of ways, but an important one is attending to personal issues between the two of you. When two people first meet, they often spend some time *pastiming*, which is nothing more than talking about such superficial things as the weather, sports, movies, and so on. Attending to how people look is another way to ease into the business at hand: "You look tired," "You seem to be harried," for example. Another rule of thumb is don't ignore the obvious. If a woman arrives at the interview clearly agitated or with tears in her eyes, it is usually a good idea to attend to it. Similarly, if a man has an obvious handicap or other infirmity that is impossible to ignore, you should consider how to acknowledge it. Nothing is funnier (in retrospect, of course) than a situation where the client knows that you are aware of some obvious characteristic that you are trying hard to ignore. You know that he knows that you know that he knows . . . etc.

Another natural dynamic when two people meet is an exploration to find their commonalities—the things they have in common. Maybe they both cheer for the same team, grew up in the same neighborhood, have children in grade school, like the same ethnic food, or hate cold weather. Finding some common ground with your clients is one way to begin connecting. This dynamic is not only important in early sessions, but can also enhance relationships later in the case management process. You will have many opportunities to share your own experiences or feelings with clients. For example, if you have experienced a loss in your family and the client is grieving about the same issue, sharing your experience could be a real support. Likewise, if a client is feeling excessively guilty about having to put his mother in a nursing home, a worker who has been through the same experience could share it as a support.

While sharing your own experiences with clients can be a support, it may also present dangerous potholes. When workers share too much or too often, clients may begin viewing the professional relationship as a friendship, which it is not. It also happens that if a worker shares feelings or incidents indicating personal vulnerability, clients try to become caregivers, switching the power dynamic of the helping relationship. This problem may be particularly apparent when an inexperienced case manager tries to balance the need to be friendly with the desire to be professional. Some supervisors state unequivocally that professionals should never divulge personal information. Most experienced case managers, however, have learned to share some personal information without diminishing their professional roles. When in doubt, check with your supervisors and colleagues. After you have been in the field for a while, you will learn to trust your own sense of yourself and to judge when sharing personal information is appropriate.

Active Listening—Restating and Reframing

One of the most important skills you will need as a case manager is that of active listening. This is the ability to track what clients are saying, what they really mean by what they are saying, and what is important to them that you understand. Two basic skills underlie active listening—*restating* and *reframing*. *Restating* is simply repeating or paraphrasing what the client has just said. It is almost as if you are a tape recorder, breaking into your client's discourse at short intervals and replaying what was just said. But the longer you wait to restate, the harder it is to remember what the client said, unless you have a very good memory! In addition, the more time there is between restating comments, the more the worker has to summarize (a different skill that we will deal with later). The effect of restating can be quite remarkable, especially when there are communication problems. Clients will hear you replay what you heard, which may or may not be what they wanted you to hear. This gives them a chance to quickly assess whether you are "getting it," and to repeat or rephrase their ideas until they are sure you understand their message. When people know they are being heard, they tend to feel more satisfied with the communication. For the case manager, successfully restating shows the client that you are really trying to understand, which allows for better contact.

Restating works particularly well when clients are trying to communicate anger, at you or at something else. Restating can keep you from becoming defensive.

Client: I'm really mad that you came in late.
Worker: I understand that you're upset because I was late.
Client: Yeah, if you can't be here on time, just let me know and I won't show up.
Worker: So you want me to let you know beforehand if I'm going to be late.
Client: Yeah!

Restating will not only make it clear to your client that you heard his anger, but will also help to defuse the anger because he knows he is being heard. This strategy works to defuse many situations where emotions run high. A caveat is in order, however. While restating is useful for assuring that clients feel they are being heard, it can backfire if used too often, creating impatience and annoyance. Used in a timely and judicious fashion, however, it is a powerful tool to improve worker-client relationships.

Reframing, the other active listening skill, can be used alone or in conjunction with restating. A reframe is a refocusing statement that is close to what the client is saying but changes or redefines it to some degree. You reframe based on what you know about your client's history, what you are aware of in the here and now, and your own experience. An example:

Client: I am so mad that caseworkers came and took my child away from me! [Tears stream down her face as she says this.]
Worker: I see that you're crying. Maybe you're sad, too.

Another example:

Client: I'm gonna run away from home and never come back! Let me tell you where I'm gonna go!
Worker: Sounds like you're mad at someone.

And again:

Client: I completely failed on my diet this weekend. After the late show on Sunday I couldn't help myself and raided the refrigerator. I'm hopeless.
Worker: You seem to be dwelling on how you failed. You were very successful on Saturday, weren't you?

In each of these cases, the worker's reframe requested that the client focus on some other aspect of what she was talking about. The reframing process is supposed to give people another way to look at what they are dealing with.

Some professionals define reframing as a way of changing a client's perception of her or his overall problem. For example, a mother with a disruptive son might blame the problem on him and want help to get him "fixed." A therapist might suggest that the boy's behavior is more of a family problem. This could also be considered a reframe. This type of reframe, though, might better be called a *psychological interpretation.* This is also a refocusing, definition-changing process, but requires workers to be well schooled in a particular theoretical construct. In the case of the disruptive child, most family therapy theories would suggest that his problems are a symptom of a more pervasive family system dynamic, so the problem should be viewed in the context of a family system reframe. This is really an interpretation, since another theory might suggest that the problem is indeed within the child. For example, if the child were diagnosed with ADHD (attention deficit, hyperactivity disorder)—a condition that some professionals believe has a physiological base—the solution would be medication. Other examples of psychological interpretations:

Client: I'm really angry at my husband. He's always trying to boss me around.

Worker: It sounds as if this is what your mother used to do with you when you were little.

Client: God, I've been so depressed since I lost my job! I don't know what to do.

Worker: Depression is really anger turned inward. Who are you angry at?

The difference between psychological interpretation and reframing is whether your responses are guided more by theoretical constructs or by your client's history, your current observations, and your own experience. Case managers do not generally use psychological interpretations in their work; they are more common in clinical casework and psychotherapy. Reframing, however, is a very useful case management tool, as it can be used to help clients refocus or redefine what they are dealing with in concrete ways.

Focusing and Furthering

The very nature of the case management interview process obliges people to tell their stories. It is in the context of these stories that case managers have to extract the kind of information that will help determine what each client requires and how best to help. But a person's need to tell stories and a worker's assessment needs are sometimes at odds with each other. When you realize that a client is digressing from what you need for assessment, you may have to use *focusing*. This skill means simply making a statement to bring the client back to the task at hand. It can be done indirectly or directly. For example:

Worker: Tell me more about your relationship with your daughter.

Client: I like her a lot, but she sure drives me crazy. She's just like my wife. The other day my wife was in the living room watching television—it was a rerun of "Dallas," you know, the one where JR gets killed. Wasn't that a great episode? I heard that more people watched it than any other . . .

Worker's indirect focusing statement:
What do you like about your daughter?
Worker direct focusing:
We're really going off the topic. Tell me about your relationship with your daughter.

Both of these focusing statements are meant to bring the client back to the topic at hand. The indirect one is more subtle, the direct one clearer about what the worker perceives and wants. Which type to use depends on how often the client gets off track. All of us digress; it becomes a problem only when someone wants communication from us that differs from what we are providing. Usually, a case manager starts with indirect focusing, then resorts to more direct focusing if necessary.

Workers should consider whether focusing is a problem for their clients. People may get annoyed if their communication pattern, their train of thought, is continually interrupted. Case managers must remember that they have two basic initial communication roles with their clients: completing the assessment task and offering emotional support. The better the relationship between client and case manager, the better focusing will work without causing irritation.

Furthering is a companion of focusing. It is the skill of helping clients continue with a topic when they are giving too little information about it. For example:

Worker: Tell me about your mother.
Client: She's mean. (pause)
Worker: What does she do that's mean?
Client: She yells at me. (pause)
Worker: What does she yell at you about?
Client: When I get in late, or don't clean up my room. (pause)
Worker: What else does she do to you that's mean?

The worker is asking the client to expand on a topic. You will notice that furthering uses open-ended questions to give a client a chance to continue without prompting.

Summarizing

Summarizing is exactly what it says. It is the skill of listening to a lot of information and synthesizing it into a few understandable statements. You are taking what the client has been saying and reducing it to a theme or concept that encapsulates the communication. Case managers may need to summarize periodically during an interview; they will almost certainly have to do so at the end of every session. Summarizing may include restating and reframing. When case managers summarize, they often start with a phrase like "It seems what you've been saying is . . ." or "Let's discuss what you've accomplished this session." Summarizing is an important skill to master because people often need help in crystallizing what they have said and what they have accomplished.

Empathy, Praise, and Support

Talking about the skills relating to empathy, praise, and support may seem to be superfluous in case management training. After all, the fact that you have decided to be a part of the helping profession should mean that you understand the need to be empathetic, offer praise, and give support. There may be truth to this, but case managers should hone these skills and be better at them than the average person.

Most people understand that empathy is the art of putting yourself in someone else's shoes, experiencing to some degree what others are feeling, and using that experience to offer support. You will notice that there are three parts to empathy: (1) the ability to imagine yourself in your client's situation, (2) feeling to some degree as he or she does, and (3) making empathetic statements. There is no way that you can relate to every painful experience that clients present. Most situations, however, offer enough corollaries from which you can find some common ground in your life experience. For example, you may not have been severely abused as a child, but you may have been spanked, humiliated, or otherwise suffered pain in your family, so you can relate to abuse situations. This gives you the basis of empathy. In many situations described by clients, you will be able to find something in your own history from which to relate.

There are times, however, when experiences are too disparate for the worker to really understand what the client is going through. Women often tell men that they just cannot understand the pain of childbirth. What they mean is that, while men obviously experience pain, it is so different from what women experience that men's expressions of empathy are less meaningful. Therefore it is often not enough for you to have found some common ground between you and a client; the client needs to perceive your experience as similar enough to hers or his in order to accept empathy from you.

Another factor in the empathy equation is your ability to actually *feel* something in relation to the client's situation. You may have some common ground but not have felt the same way about it. If you experienced the loss of a parent with whom you were very close, while your client lost a hated parent and is experiencing relief, you obviously have two different feelings stemming from similar events. Another circumstance arises when people have had similar experiences from opposite sides. If you were sexually abused as a child and are working with a perpetrator, your feelings about an abusive relationship will of course be very different from your client's.

The moral of these stories is: Don't expect that you will feel empathy in all client situations. There is no rule in the helping professions that says you should. And even when you do feel empathy, don't expect that all clients will be able to accept it. When you do empathize, however, show it. Empathetic communications start with appropriate facial expressions and tones of voice. You need to *look* and *sound* concerned. You should also express what the commonality is between you.

More often than not, people sense it when a worker's attempts at empathy are not based on real common experiences and feelings. Children have particularly good antennae that pick up occasions when professionals are being phony. In such situations, it is usually a good idea to let clients know that you are concerned about their pain but are having a hard time relating to it because it is so foreign to your experience. People usually relate positively to honesty, especially when it comes with a show of concern and a wish to stay connected. If you really do empathize but are rebuffed, don't get defensive by trying to convince your client of your good intentions. Rather, use active listening skills and continue to show concern; there may come a time when your empathy will be accepted.

Praise, or positive support, is also an important part of the case management process. Providing it is as much an art as it is a science. Positive support in case management serves two different purposes, and one does not necessarily affect the other. In many instances, it is just a natural, spontaneous response to what a client is saying or has accomplished. The only expectation about this type of communication is that it will enhance a good client-worker relationship.

In other circumstances positive support may be used to help clients do something, like show up at referral sources or learn to manage their problems for themselves. Research from behavior therapy suggests that for positive support to stimulate new behavior patterns, it should be viewed as valuable to the receiver, given with appropriate intensity, and offered soon after the behavior it is trying to support. Paradoxically, once a new behavior pattern has been established, the frequency of positive support should be significantly decreased in order for the pattern to be maintained. Thus when workers use support in this way, they need to pay special attention to how and when they praise or smile. For example, the use of contingent praise has helped children behave appropriately during interviews, learn how to answer questions, and control anger. Specialized training is available to help workers learn more about how and when contingent support is appropriate, and how to make it effective in helping clients to attain their goals (Whaley & Mallott, 1996).

An aspect of positive support is knowing how to turn a negative into a positive. Whenever clients say something negative about themselves, workers can always reframe a positive side. For example:

Client: I tried to play baseball, but I couldn't do it.
Worker: You really tried to do something that's hard to learn, even if it didn't work out. A lot of people don't even try. Good for you!

Client: I'm so depressed, I stay in bed all day and never leave my house.

Worker: You came here today—that shows you're making some progress.

Client: I've tried to stop drinking again and again, and I always fail.

Worker: The fact that you keep trying puts you way ahead of people who try once and never try again. That shows a good deal of courage.

Client: I feel very guilty about putting my retarded son into an institution. I feel like I failed.

Worker: I know you do. It's very hard to give him up after all the years you had him at home. Tell me something about the things you taught him to do when he was growing up.

No matter when or how you choose to use positive support, it is essential, as it was with empathy, that it be done honestly, sincerely, and with conviction. Remember, most people can spot phoniness a mile away.

Setting Boundaries

You are setting boundaries when you tell someone what you can tolerate and cannot tolerate about his or her behavior; what about him or her you like and don't like; or how the two of you are the same and dissimilar. This is a skill that is also important in case management relationships with clients, supervisors, administrators, and community contacts. For instance, it is quite common to explain to clients during their first interviews what rules—also known as agency norms—are connected with receiving service from your agency. These norms may begin with the need to arrive on time for appointments, to call twenty-four hours in advance to cancel, to pay fees if appropriate, and to follow through on agreements when they are made. Whenever boundaries are set, compliance is usually improved when the consequences for compliance and noncompliance are made explicit. There are times, however, when negative consequences become clear only when the rule is broken. For instance, when a client starts habitually coming late for appointments, you will have to explain the consequences if the behavior continues.

A number of assertive skills accompany boundary setting: the ability to say no; the ability to make requests and demands; and the ability to express feelings such as irritation, annoyance, and anger. All of us have surfeits and deficits with assertive skills, depending on the situations and people involved. There are many ways to let people know they are not meeting others' expectations, ranging on a continuum from gentle, corrective feedback to demanding, angry feedback. Everyone working in the helping professions needs to have skills all along this continuum.

While none of us like to be told that our behavior is unacceptable, it is an important part of communication in relationships, including professional relationships. When giving corrective feedback to a client (or anyone, for that matter), it is very important to keep three things in mind. First, you need to focus on people's *behavior*, not on perceived characteristics of their personalities.

For example:

- Your coming late to appointments is a problem. NOT: Your laziness is a problem.

- Your outbursts of anger cannot continue here. NOT: Your hostile personality is a problem here.

- You are not showing up for AA meetings, and we need to deal with this. NOT: Missing AA meetings shows how inadequate you are, and we have to deal with it.

Second, you need to make it clear where the *sanctions* concerning unacceptable behavior are coming from. For example, take a recovering client who wants to return to his friendship network that included the use of drugs:

- *General experience or theoretical basis:* Experience has shown that when you engage in this behavior, it's a trigger for you to backslide. When people do this, it makes them sicker.

- *Personal:* Your behavior is creating a problem for me.

- *Interpersonal:* When you engage in this behavior, it usually turns people off. It may create a problem for you in your group.

- *Agency:* Your behavior is violating an agency rule.

- *Community:* This behavior is against the law.

Third, you need to let the client know the *consequences* of continued unacceptable behavior. You may want to stress personal disappointment, agency consequences, or consequences in the community.

One of the reasons it is helpful to have a supportive relationship with clients (or supervisors, administrators, or community contacts) is that it is easier to hear corrective feedback from someone you like and/or respect. When there is a sense of trust, the communication of irritation followed by a firm request or demand is likely to be taken seriously. Case managers face many different situations where they need to set very firm boundaries with strong assertive skills, no matter what the practice setting. Such situations arise when a client begins to threaten you or someone else; when a client arrives "high" for an appointment; when you find out that a client is about to commit a crime, is abusing a child, or is considering suicide; and when you learn that other professionals are acting inappropriately with clients.

It is often hard to know how strongly you should establish a boundary and how assertive you should be. Case managers constantly worry about alienating clients or other professionals when they set boundaries, especially when the situations aren't clear-cut. Your goal is always to communicate your displeasure professionally in ways that don't alienate people, although this is not always possible. Experience is the best teacher in this regard. After some boundary-setting experiences—whether with clients, supervisors, agency administrators, or community people—you will feel that you should have acted differently. Use supervision and collegial relationships to process these incidents. *All* case managers, including those with years of experience, can tell war stories about difficult boundary-setting experiences in their practice.

Along with setting boundaries, there is a corollary skill that sometimes helps—the ability to accept negative feedback yourself, both from clients and from other professionals. Being comfortable accepting negative feedback about your behavior has a number of positive benefits. The better you are able to do it, the more successful you will be in defusing potentially annoying and sometimes volatile situations. You will often find that you can learn something important about yourself and others if you can really listen. Active listening skills are at the core of accepting negative feedback. Active listening allows you to process what is being said without becoming defensive; it also gives the other person a chance to let you know how he or she feels, which is very important.

After you have heard the negative feedback, the next step, depending on the person and situation, may be negotiation or contracting, skills that we will cover shortly.

For the Teacher or Trainer
Optional Exercises for Chapter 5

Many of these exercises are designed for two-person role-plays, usually with one student as a worker and the other as a client. (You will be asking them to pair up and choose roles.) Students in the client role can base their role-play on clients from their worksites, people they know (without identifiers), or their own personal experiences. It is not necessary for students playing the client to inform the "worker" about the basis for their role-playing.

1. Diversity issues

Have students choose a partner. Ask them to discuss diversity issues involving sexual, racial, cultural, ethnic, and religious differences. Then ask them to explore how they differ in terms of family history, where they have lived and live now, significant life experiences, education, and socioeconomic background. Finally, lead a group discussion to elicit what they found hard, what they found easy, and if what they experienced relates to their work with clients.

2. First impressions

Have students choose a partner whom they do not know, or do not know well. Ask each pair to have a ten-minute conversation on any subject they choose, such as where they like to go on vacation, movies they have enjoyed, current events, and so on. Then ask them to give each other feedback about the most salient first impressions they formed. Finally, lead a group discussion, asking whether what they heard was expected or different from their own perceptions of themselves. What did they learn from this exercise that could be related to their first meetings with clients, from both their perspective and the client's perspective?

3. Taking notes and staying in contact

Ask students to pair up and choose roles. They should have paper and a pen. Ask the student in the client role to tell a story about some problem for ten minutes. The student in the worker role should take good notes about this problem and about their worker-client interaction. When the time is up, they should switch roles and repeat the exercise. When they have completed this role-play, ask them to discuss with each other how they as clients would rate their workers in terms of contact. Then lead a group discussion focusing on (1) the difficulties workers had staying in contact and taking notes, and (2) ideas about how to achieve and maintain better contact.

4. Asking questions

Have students form groups of three. One will be a client, one a worker, and one an observer. There will be three five-minute scenarios. After each one, students will switch roles so that each will have a chance to play all three.

Ask the client to talk about any problem for five minutes. The worker should (1) ask open-ended questions, (2) ask closed-ended questions, and (3) make information-seeking statements instead of asking questions. On a piece of paper, the observer should write three headings: open-ended questions, closed-ended questions, and statements asking for information. During each five-minute scenario, the student observer should put a check mark in the appropriate column whenever the worker carries out one of the three. After all students have had their turns, ask them to share their observer data with each other. Have them discuss their styles of getting information, which types of questions/statements they tended to emphasize, how they as clients felt about the questioning styles, and the effects the questioning styles might have on actual clients. Then lead a class discussion about what students learned from this exercise.

Another way to do this is to ask two students to role-play in front of the class, or show a tape of an initial interview if you have one. Ask each student watching to be an observer, recording with check marks in the appropriate columns. Then lead a group discussion similar to the one above.

5. Attending to the obvious

Describe the following situations to the group, one at a time. (1) The client arrives smelling very bad. (2) The client arrives walking with an obvious limp. (3) The client has a large and disfiguring birthmark on his face. (4) The client arrives wearing outrageous clothes or is clearly dressed too skimpily. Then lead a discussion about what students should do (if anything) in each of these circumstances if they occurred (a) during initial interviews, and (b) after they have known the client for some time. After this discussion, ask students if they have ever had similar experiences with actual clients.

6. Personal disclosure

Lead a discussion about what students think is appropriate as far as telling clients about their personal lives. Since this issue is driven by practice wisdom, certain theoretical foundations, and the differing norms established by agencies, you should share your own opinion with the class. Among the questions you might ask: What are the issues in revealing yourself to a client? What are the possible positive and negative consequences? How much of this issue is due to personal style? What do major theories of helping say about this issue? What should workers do if their own style or preference about personal disclosure is significantly different from what their agency expects?

7. *Active listening and interviewing skills*

The skills that can be practiced as part of active listening and interviewing are restating, reframing, focusing, furthering, and summarizing. Each of them can be practiced alone or in combination. For students with less experience, we recommend that each be practiced one at a time before being combined with others. The following exercise is set up in this way, but can be easily modified for any skill combination. Ask students to pair up and choose roles. The student client should talk about anything for five to ten minutes, depending on how much time you have. The student worker should practice using one skill, such as restating. After this first period is finished, the students should switch roles and repeat the exercise. Then lead a class discussion about what happened in their role-plays and the use of the requisite skill in actual practice.

8. *Empathy, praise, and reframing negatives to positives*

Use the same role-play model as in #7. Again, you will need to decide whether to ask students to practice one skill at a time or use them in combination. For example, the worker could spend the entire period making empathy statements, or could practice all three skills. Many students need practice reframing client negative statements into positive ones. It is a help in these situations if student clients make particularly deprecating and negative statements.

9. *Using contingent support*

Contingent support techniques will probably be needed by students or trainees working with mentally retarded citizens, the chronically mentally ill, mentally disabled geriatric clients, and emotionally disturbed children. Ask students to pair up and choose roles. Then set up a situation where the student client needs to learn a specific skill. For example, he or she could role-play a boy who is continually jumping out of his seat. The student worker could then practice "catch a kid doing something good" by focusing on the boy when he is sitting down. Another scenario might have the student client role-play a mentally retarded woman who is trying to learn to put on her coat by herself or figure out how to read street signs. After these role-plays, discuss the difficulties involved and the importance of concrete, clear, and immediate contingent support.

10. Setting boundaries

The basic skills behind setting boundaries with clients, colleagues, supervisors, and other professionals are the ability to say no, the ability to make requests and demands, and the ability to express feelings. There are many simulations for practicing these skills, and the following are only representative. In all these examples, ask students to pair up and choose roles.

A. *The ability to say no.* Ask the student clients to try to persuade a student worker to do one of the following: spend social time with the client outside the agency setting; divulge some personal information that is clearly inappropriate; give the client bus fare to save him a long walk home.

B. *The ability to make requests.* Ask student workers to request that a client start showing up on time; stop being abusive to others in a group; or start paying a managed care $5.00 co-pay fee.

This skill can also be practiced on the organizational level. This time one student plays the worker and the other a supervisor. Ask workers to request that the supervisor give them more time for supervision; be less critical and more supportive; give them a raise.

C. *The ability to express feelings.* Instruct workers to let their clients know that they are angry about one of the following behaviors: constantly missing appointments; constantly coming in late; attacking another client; threatening the worker or other staff members with physical harm.

11. Giving corrective feedback

Ask students to pair up and choose roles. Instruct the workers to tell their clients one or more of the following: what the worker doesn't like about the client's abusive verbal behavior during their sessions and with other clients; that the client is being taken advantage of by friends because he or she is too unassertive; that the client is partly responsible for her or his child's acting-out behavior at home and school; that the worker is not happy with the client-worker relationship and wants to suggest ways in which the client could improve it. This skill too can be practiced at the organizational level, with one student as worker and the other as supervisor. Ask the workers to tell their supervisors what they don't like about the supervision sessions and what they would like to see changed. Another option is for one role to be that of a worker and the other that of a professional in another agency. Instruct the workers to (a) tell the other professional that they do not like what has been happening with the referrals made to that agency, and (b) suggest that they try to find out what can be done.

12. Accepting negative feedback

Ask students to pair up and choose roles. Instruct the clients to criticize the workers for certain behaviors. (Clients can get angry if they feel that it fits in their role-play.) Workers should practice active listening.

In another scenario, have one student play the worker and the other her or his supervisor. The supervisor should criticize the worker about his or her work; the worker should practice active listening.

6 Specialized Practice Skills

Several specialized skills have been identified as applicable at different points in the case management process. The most important are determining eligibility; the psycho-social assessment; methods of problem identification; establishing problem severity; hypothesis development; and goal setting.

Determining Eligibility

At first glance, determining whether potential clients have the characteristics that will allow them to enter your case management system seems to be a simple matter. All you need is a list of eligibility criteria and the ability to ask the right questions. Unfortunately, even after case managers have answered eligibility questions, they are often still uncertain about whether clients should receive services or be referred elsewhere. People's problems are often multifaceted, and do not easily fit into simple diagnostic slots.

All social service agencies attempt to place people into previously established categories to determine eligibility. They do this for many reasons. Funding streams often mandate service for selected problem areas; in a managed care environment, agencies can treat only selected diagnoses; some agencies tend to specialize in specific types of clients or problem areas; new diagnostic categories crop up as research and practice define problems differently. Suppose you are working in a case management program specializing in drug addictions and you see a client who you suspect also has a chronic mental illness—a so-called MICA (Mentally Ill Chemically Addicted) client. Should he be referred to a case management program specializing in MICA problems, referred to a mental health program, or remain in your program? Since many addicted clients could easily be given a mental health diagnosis based on the Diagnostic and Statistical Manual-4 (DSM-IV-TR), at what point should clients with mental illnesses be considered MICA? Another issue: Case managers may want to refer clients to managed care services. But some managed care programs will not cover the DSM-IV-TR "V-codes," which include "normal" life-cycle problems such as marital conflict and parent-child difficulties. If a couple is in desperate need of marital therapy, case managers may need to come up with an additional DSM-IV-TR diagnosis that is insurable, so that the husband and wife will be eligible for marital counseling.

Case management administrators and supervisors are critically aware of the problems relating to eligibility determination, so case managers can expect to receive a good deal of training and support in this area. There will probably be times when you will disagree with others in your agency about a client's eligibility; at such times it will be helpful to remember that determining eligibility can be somewhat of an art form, with decisions based on subjective criteria.

Assessment—The Psycho-Social

There are two important skill phases in case management assessment. The first requires information-gathering skills, which in social services is often called the psycho-social process. The second phase requires analysis skills of the psycho-social data to develop hypotheses about what factors are causing clients' problems.

The psycho-social has a long tradition in social services. It is a document that comes out of the first stage of the helping process, summarizing what has been learned about the client, together with indications of future directions. While the concept of the psychosocial is universal, its format is not. Agencies develop their own psycho-social reporting systems, with different outlines and forms. In its most traditional form, the psycho-social is done in a narrative style, usually in two to three single-spaced typed pages. What follows is a sample psycho-social outline. Remember, however, that you will need to follow the format dictated by the agency in which you work. A general psycho-social outline has a number of components. While this sample covers all areas, you or your agency may or may not be interested in specific items within each topic.

Basic demographic information: Client name, address, phone number, birth date, age, sex, marital status; place of employment with address and phone number, other means of income; educational attainment. Names and relationships of relevant family members, with all of the above information, including school information for children.

Personal history information: Place of birth; family of origin history, including information about parents, siblings, early childhood family dynamics, and any remarkable health and interactional incidents that occurred when growing up. Pay special attention to parenting patterns and who acted as caregivers, and note any family history of separation and divorce, alcohol or drug addiction, health problems, and physical or sexual abuse. Family behavior during children's adolescence is often of interest, and ways in which children separated from the family may also be important. Conclude this section with a description of the current family situation.

Presenting problem history: Track the history of the presenting problem—when it started, who was involved, how the client and family coped, what social services have been involved, the circumstances under which they were contacted, the interventions used over time, and the outcomes of these interventions. Describe the severity of the problem behavior over time, any patterns that are evident, and the situations in which there was some improvement or regression.

Current state of the problem behavior: Describe in some detail what happened that brought the client to you, the current situation, and what other social services or community organizations are involved.

Current needs, immediate plans: When you do an initial psychosocial, you may not have had enough time to conduct a complete assessment of what is causing the problem and what needs to be done about it. But the end of the psycho-social should include whatever you do know at this point and whatever immediate plans are being made to help a client.

There are many suggested formats to guide your questions so that you don't miss an important area. Your agency will probably have developed a format to fit its requirements, but guidelines generally cover the following areas:

Drug and alcohol use
Physical health
Mental health
Life skills
Parenting skills (when applicable)
Housing
Education
Employment
Income
Money management
Nutrition
Marital, family dynamics
Literacy
Recreation
Use of community resources
Religious/ethnic involvement
Friendship and extended family involvement

It is customary for psycho-socials to be typed and placed in client records. They are used to review cases and are often sent to referral agencies, with appropriate client consent.

Methods of Problem Identification

Case managers always need to identify one or more problem areas when clients arrive for service. By the very nature of each agency, at least one problem may be assumed—child abuse, for instance, or a health problem or a need for welfare. For better or worse, many clients you see will be categorized by some type of label. Hopefully, it will be useful in directing intervention strategies, obtaining public assistance, or at least getting third-party insurance reimbursement. There are many ways of defining problems. For example, there are comprehensive labeling methods for clients with mental, physical, or legal problems. Case managers working in the mental health arena have to gain familiarity with the DSM-IV-TR, which is published by the American Psychiatric Association. Because it categorizes every known problem behavior in the area of mental health, it is used extensively to diagnose clients. Similarly, case managers in health settings need to become familiar with medical diagnoses assigned by physicians. Likewise, workers involved with forensic issues have to know the wide range of labeling categories used in criminal proceedings. Case managers can also define problems in terms of service deficits. This means that clients' problems are defined in terms of what they lack, such as housing, welfare, employment, education, or health services. Thus a homeless client's immediate problem can be defined as a need to be connected with a social service agency that finds appropriate housing. It is also possible to define a problem as a lack of involvement with natural community resources — family connections, religious institutions, community centers, volunteer networks, or recreational opportunities.

You can thus view client problems at three possible levels: the personal and interpersonal, in terms of service deficits, and as a lack of community involvement. No matter what problem identification system case managers use, they should also provide examples of what labels mean. Problems should be defined behaviorally, either in terms of what the client is specifically doing (observable), thinking (cognitive), or feeling (emotional) or in terms of how severe a service deprivation is. You also need to explain specifically how the problem is affecting the client, client system, or community. Describing some recent events to further explain problems can be of help as well.

Establishing Problem Severity

Once problems have been defined, case managers need to estimate their severity. This is more than just an academic exercise. With the large caseloads that are common in most case management systems, establishing problem severity is a critical skill that determines how soon the worker should deal with a client's needs. Estimating problem severity by acquiring good initial baseline information helps in the evaluation of case management services. It also allows both clients and workers to track goal attainment over time.

Assessing problem severity often just requires using common sense. If adults or children are in danger of serious physical, emotional, or sexual abuse, their situation is obviously critical. If it is clear that there is an impending situation that will cause a family crisis—the loss of benefits, a home, or a job—this, too, is serious. In assessment, much of the time you will take what clients say at face value; at other times you will receive reports before meeting them; in still other situations, you may have to confirm independently what a client has told you.

For some presenting problems there are standardized behavioral indicators that can help to assess problem severity. For example, there are questionnaires that assess the severity of depression, suicidal ideations, and phobic responses. Other tests ask workers to record their observations about children's social behavior, level of aggression, and preschool academic readiness. For the most part, however, these tests require some degree of training and so are not frequently used in case management programs.

Many case management programs make use of baseline behavioral indicators that can be documented. These can be as simple as subjective 5-point rating systems, in which a 5 indicates that a problem is very severe and a 1 means that there is no problem behavior at all. Here are some examples of possible baseline behaviors from different case management programs:

Drugs and alcohol	Number of times drug used per day over the last month
Homeless	Number of days spent on the street in the last year
Mental retardation	Number of times child dresses himself/herself per week
Chronic mental illness	Number of times attended day treatment in last six months

Forensic	Number and type of crimes committed in last year
Child abuse	Number of incidents reported in last year
Spousal abuse	Number of times victim reported abuse in last month
Welfare	Monthly family income over last six months
Workfare	Number of days worked in last year

You will notice from these examples that they represent attempts to find countable and observable behavioral indicators. These indicators do not necessarily show the breadth or depth of a problem area. They are, as the term implies, *indicators;* if the problem is substantially ameliorated, the indicator should show it. The opposite could also happen; the indicator would show improvement, but the basic problem would still be present. For example, an alcoholic could stop drinking, but not participate in or complete a comprehensive treatment program. In the addiction world, he or she is called a "dry alcoholic," suggesting that the problem is not really being dealt with.

Hypothesis Development

When all is said and done, the core of case management assessment is to develop a hypothesis concerning *why* a problem is occurring. All of the information you collect is supposed to lead you to this point. A good hypothesis dictates goals and intervention plans. Often the reasons behind a problem are patently obvious— a lack of money, opportunity, or resources. Case managers don't need a lot of training to assess that the basic reason why children are malnourished is that they don't have enough food to eat, or that the reason an addicted man commits petty theft is to support his habit. Both hypotheses would dictate interventions: obtain food support and drug treatment, respectively. However, life is too complex to assume that the reasons why things happen are so simple. Good assessment skills require more than the ability to ask good questions when collecting psycho-social information. Assessment at this stage challenges the worker's ability to categorize and process this information in ways that will explain *why* problems occur, taking into consideration a broader systems perspective.

Clearly, many problems must be immediately dealt with regardless of their causes. Children who are abused must be separated from abusers; people who commit crimes need to be restrained from doing so; families who are hungry must be fed. There are agencies and other community resources that can respond to these immediate problems. But these and other crisis interventions may not lead to a permanent solution. A mother's abuse of her son is not necessarily solved by separating the two. *Why* is this abuse occurring? Is it because of an addiction, mental illness, or lack of parenting skills? Is it because the woman is working hard to support her family and has no child support? Is it related to the stress of being unemployed or having too little money to support her family adequately? Could it have to do with discrimination or social isolation? Or is it some combination of these factors? Each hypothesis would dictate a different type of intervention. This is the challenge of assessment.

It is sad but true that assessment skills are much clearer at the personal and interpersonal levels than at the organizational, community, and political levels. This is probably because the complexity of human interactions greatly increases as more people and institutions are thrown into the assessment pot. However, case managers should not be deterred from working on their assessment skills just because assessment may be difficult. Remember, what you want to end up with is a reasonable *hypothesis* underlying a problem. A hypothesis is not supposed to reflect certainty. By definition, it is your best interpretation of the information you have collected. The best proof of a hypothesis comes from testing it out. If your hypothesis is correct, the client should show long-term improvement in identified problem areas. If there is little or no change, you will need to re-evaluate. An inappropriate hypothesis may be one reason why a goal has not been reached or maintained.

Assessment at the personal/interpersonal level is supported by any number of psychological theories. In the behavioral approach, such as behavior and cognitive-behavior therapies, the reason a behavior occurs is the consequences that follow it. To put it succinctly, all behaviors occur because they are reinforced. A mother abuses her child because she receives reinforcement for doing so. Psychodynamic theories, such as ego psychology and object relations theory, suggest that early childhood experiences are at the root of all personal and interpersonal problems. Therefore, the reason why a mother abuses her child lies in her history, to be uncovered and "cleansed" through therapy. Family systems theories, such as the structural approaches, hold that family dynamics explain why people act as they do. In this formulation, the reason why a mother abuses her child lies in the ways she and others in her family system interact and support each other.

The point of such theories is that they direct the worker toward a hypothesis suggesting a method of intervention. These theoretical formulations are used mainly by clinical social workers, psychiatric nurses, and psychologists in agencies that provide therapy. Their direct use in case management assessment is not a central focus unless therapy is part of the case management system.

As we stated earlier, systems theory is at the heart of case management assessment. While some modern psychological theories incorporate the concepts and ideas of systems theory, their formulations are bounded by the individual or the family. Still, it is helpful if case managers have some basic knowledge of individual and interpersonal theories as they assess these dynamics in relation to larger systems. One way to see how a client's psychological makeup interacts with larger systems is to observe the dynamics of the professional case management relationship. Useful indicators include how clients react to stress, perceive reality, interact with you and others, and process information.

We should be careful not to become so enamored of individual and family system theories that we forget the impact of organizational, community, political, and cultural systems on every client. While case managers need to carefully assess psychological variables, they must remember that there are also larger systems interacting with client problems. It is all too easy to assume that everybody needs to be referred for therapy, no matter what the problem. Therapy may be important as part of a long-term solution for a client, but it is not always indicated. The client below, a recent immigrant from a Third World country that does not have a psychotherapeutic tradition, was referred for traditional psychotherapy to treat stress relating to job loss.

Worker: It appears that you are under a lot of stress.
Client: I just lost my job, and I'm behind in my rent. Why am I here?
Worker: Therapy can help you cope better with your situation.
Client: I don't need therapy; I need a job.

(As Sigmund Freud, the father of psychoanalysis, is purported to have said, "Sometimes a cigar is just a cigar!") Some problems are best resolved by dealing directly with what triggered them. In this case, the client might have been better served by help in finding work or a job retraining program.

Assessing client behavior in relation to organizational, community, and political issues is as important as psychological assessment but without as clear a theoretical roadmap. Systems theory instructs us that many issues, called *structural issues,* interact with every problem in our lives. Structural issues have to do with what happens in people's lives due to their involvement, or lack thereof, with institutions and the community. From the perspective of systems theory, it is impossible to separate personal/interpersonal variables and the structural issues in our lives. Understanding this interaction is essential in understanding why problems occur.

To assess the impact of structural issues, a case manager needs a good knowledge base about client presenting problems. This knowledge comes from experience and research. With this base, case managers can ask the types of questions that will support a broader systems hypothesis. For example, it is known that child abuse can be correlated with a number of factors, each of which would dictate different interventions. A worker could emerge from the assessment process with the following intervention grid:

Reasons Why Parents Abuse Children	Levels of Possible Interventions			
	Psychological	Organizational	Community	Political
Parental history of abuse	X			
Lack of parenting skills		X	X	
Chronic unemployment			X	X
Social isolation	X		X	
Economic deprivation			X	X
Lack of child care		X	X	X
Racial/ethnic discrimination			X	
Children's mental illness	X	X		
Parents' mental illness	X	X		
Addictions	X	X	X	X
Divorce/family dysfunction	X	X	X	
Health problems		X	X	

Each of these areas brings into focus different issues that might contribute to child abuse. According to one cliché, "it takes a village to raise a child." The implication is that when parents need support in rearing their children, it can come only from neighbors and from such community institutions as schools and community centers. Similarly, children who suffer from serious behavioral disorders, such as ADHD, present even good parents with tremendous challenges. This disorder may have not only psychological determinants but also physiological bases, and both may be exacerbated by the failure of schools to adequately diagnose and deal with the problem. It is well known that child abuse is common when parents suffer from alcohol addiction. In this case, dealing with the addiction becomes a primary goal, with questions raised about the quality of prior treatment (when it has occurred), how the community views addiction, and how alcoholism is supported politically (through laws regarding its availability and the minimal sanctions for its abuse). Since so many issues are connected to how our society allocates resources to support children and families, one could make a good case for suggesting that political dynamics should *always* be considered when assessing child abuse cases.

Another assessment issue that should be considered is the possible failure of previous interventions. This is particularly true in the case management of addictions. Often, addicted clients have been through treatment programs before being referred to you. While the clients certainly bear some responsibility for their recovery, it is also true that the quality of treatment programs differs considerably in this country.

When research or knowledge is lacking, the practice wisdom of seasoned case managers is another resource to draw upon. Developing assessment hypotheses can be as much of an art as a science. The requisite skills are best learned by practice, by evaluating results through supervision, and by program evaluation.

Goal Setting

Setting goals is an essential part of case management; it allows for worker and client accountability and adds clarity about what is expected over time. Case management uses two kinds of goals, behavioral goals and service goals. Behavioral goals are based on what is supposed to change in clients' behavior over time; service goals focus on what connections clients have to make in order to meet their needs. These two types of goals are often closely linked, with one dependent on another. Goal-setting skills include behavioral specificity, turning negative goals into positive ones, and partializing.

Specific goals in case management are sometimes obvious: A client needs to obtain welfare benefits; find housing; get a job; immunize the family; stay off drugs or alcohol. However, whenever a change in behavior is part of a goal, the question arises of how specifically behavior should be labeled. For example, you could say that the client's goal is to improve "ego strengths," or self-esteem, or coping skills. Conceptually, there is nothing wrong with these goals, but how would anyone know when they had been reached? The issue, then, is to define behavioral goals in such a way as to make it reasonably clear when they have been attained. One way to do this is to define the behavior that would result when the goal has been reached. In the case of a chronically mentally ill man who needs to develop ego strengths, the goals might be (a) to make at least two new friends, and (b) to complete three projects he likes. An improvement in self-esteem for an unemployed mother might be tied to (a) finishing a job-training course, and (b) expressing positive ideas about her future. A drug addict could demonstrate better coping skills by (a) expressing anger appropriately, (b) contracting more effectively for what he needs from his wife and children, (c) staying off drugs for a month, and (d) telling ten stories about how he has avoided addictive "triggers."

The trick to setting good behavioral goals is to achieve the right descriptive balance between general issues and behavioral specificity. The worker should describe how the situation should look at termination, with enough clarity so that goal attainment can be quantified. Thus, setting a goal for a depressed client that her depression will be under control in three months is generally descriptive, but does not specify clearly what this might mean. The goal might also specify that she will be sleeping no more than eight hours a day, be taking her anti-depression medication as prescribed, and be attending weekly therapy 90 percent of the time.

A second skill in the goal-setting process involves negative versus positive goals. Examples of negative goals are to decrease drug or alcohol addictive behavior; to stop abusing children; to decrease violent behavior; to cease criminal activity; or to decrease schizophrenic episodes. There is nothing inherently wrong with any of these goals, but note their common theme: All of them require that clients stop doing something, but none of them suggest an alternative appropriate goal. In some cases the positive goal is implied, but in many others it should be clearly specified. Thus an alcoholic client at case management termination should show decreasing addictive behavior—that is, abstinence. Also, should he be attending AA five times a week, attending weekly treatment sessions, have completed a job-training program, and be actively seeking a job. The general rule of thumb in goal setting is that whenever a negative goal is specified, there should be at least one accompanying positive goal aimed at an appropriate alternative behavior. Society itself (as well as social service workers) is quick to point out what we should *not* be doing. It is much more difficult to indicate what we *should* be doing instead.

A third essential skill for good case management practice is *partializing*. This means taking an apparently unsolvable big problem and breaking it into little solvable pieces. Many problems appear to be insurmountable to people as they present them. Indeed, the complexity of client problems can initially appear to be intimidating even to case managers. It is always possible, however, to begin a partializing process with any issue so that reasonable short-term goals can be established. In the behavioral approach this process is called *shaping,* or the art of successive approximations. A series of small and doable behavioral goals is set, each of which helps further movement to an important long-term goal.

There is no right or wrong way to break down problems and set up approximation goals; often it is more an art than a science. For example, if you want to go to St. Louis from New York City, you can travel along many different roads. Some may be faster, some more scenic. Sometimes you stop for awhile to rest; sometimes you run into unexpected detours. What is most important is that you always move in the general direction of St. Louis. It is the same with taking a client's long-term behavioral goal and breaking it down into successive component parts, all of which take you toward the terminal goal.

Let us assume that you are working as a case manager in an addictions program. Your client, Meg, is an alcoholic. She has a history of starting outpatient treatment, going to Alcoholics Anonymous, being successful for a short time, and then falling off the wagon again. She is depressed and feels hopeless about ever maintaining sobriety. She lives alone, has worked part time on and off for the last year, has few friends she can count on, no relatives, and no community connections. She is currently receiving SSI.

Abstinence is an obvious long-term goal. Just as in planning the trip to St. Louis, you face an infinite number of possible successive approximations to help Meg get there. Good assessment should suggest what these could be. You have hypothesized that her social and community supports have been historically inadequate to sustain her sobriety. If you define the immediate goals in the direction of support issues, her problem may seem more manageable to Meg, even if she doesn't see their applicability to her goal of sobriety. You would begin an intensive process of partializing: (1) For the first week, Meg would agree to come to the day treatment agency. Concurrently, she would agree to a daily community visit, with you or a mentor, choosing among a local church pastor of her choice, the YWCA, a woman's self-help support group, and three organizations looking for volunteers. (2) During the second week, Meg would continue attending the day treatment program, and would choose at least three places to visit a second time, with you or her mentor. (3) During the third week, Meg would continue attending day treatment and commit to at least two community activities for the next month.

What is clear about partializing Meg's problems and goals in this way is that she will need a lot of support from you on each step of her journey. We know several things about the shaping process. First, each approximation needs immediate and intense support before the next one is undertaken. Second, too little support for an approximation will increase the likelihood that a client will regress back to old habits. Third, inconsistent support will probably result in inconsistent client compliance. Fourth, an approximation that is too hard should be broken up into even smaller steps.

When a client is not moving in the right direction, or if she is regressing, you can view her behavior in two ways. You can assume that she is unmotivated and resistant, and try to deal with her on an intra-psychic level. Or you can assume that her environmental support is inadequate. In most cases, people get stuck because of a combination of both factors—a lack of motivation and an inadequate support system   .
Perhaps these two issues are really two sides of the same coin. In any case, there is no question that people need support in order to change, and that how and when that support is offered is critical in making small steps to big goals.

It is also true that people need "self-support" to help them meet their needs. Self-support is especially important when support from others is not available or forthcoming. But the ability to support oneself is a learned skill like any other. Almost by definition, most of the people who come to case management agencies for help need to develop better self-support skills. Therefore, to expect people who are vulnerable and in pain to rely mainly on themselves is setting them up for failure. The reality for most of us is that we learn new skills most efficiently when we get a mix of support from others and from ourselves. When either is lacking, we rely more heavily on the other one. So it is with our clients.

Effective goal setting in general, like any difficult skill, is one that requires training, time, and experience. Because case management goals include both behavioral and service components, setting them can be complex. Like their clients, case management trainees should not allow themselves to be intimidated by seemingly insurmountable long-term training goals. They should partialize by setting up appropriate approximations for each major professional skill area, and make sure they get adequate support from themselves, their colleagues, and their supervisors.

For the Teacher or Trainer
Optional Exercises for Chapter 6

Some of the topics covered here have appeared with earlier chapters; they involve the more advanced skills that need to be practiced and learned at this stage.

1. Psycho-social

Ask students to pair up and choose roles. If you have access to relevant psycho-social outlines from agency-based practice, use them. Otherwise, use the outline in this chapter. The student worker should conduct a psycho-social interview with the student client for twenty to thirty minutes. Students should then discuss how the process worked for them as both worker and client.

2. Hypothesis development during assessment

Ask students to present cases with the following outline: a description of relevant psycho-social information; identified problems; goals; and a hypothesis about causation, using the three system levels—micro, mezzo, and macro. They should then discuss the direction interventions should take, what interventions are possible and reasonable, and what interventions are not and why.

3. Goal setting

A. Do one of the following: present a case to your students focusing on one problem area and goal; or ask students to use a case of their own, focusing on one problem area and goal. Ask students to develop a list of at least five clear approximations, or intermediate goals, that will support the client in reaching the final goal. Ask students to present their series of intermediate goals and use group discussion to evaluate how well they did this.

B. Ask a student to volunteer, and send her out of the room beyond earshot. Tell the class that they will try to "shape" the student's behavior—going to the blackboard and picking up an eraser, or something similar—with the starting point being at the door when she returns to the room. Ask the volunteer to return and stand by the door. At this time, tell her that whenever she hears a hand clap, she should imagine that it is worth a dollar, so she should try to get as many dollars (hand claps) as possible. The group must then collectively and nonverbally figure out the approximations they will want to support with their applause in order for her to reach her goal. The first approximations should be walking toward the blackboard, then nearing the eraser, and finally grasping the eraser. (This simulation is like the cold-hot game children play, but without a cue for "cold.")

What students should look for as they clap are the following: (1) When they clap too much, the subject will literally become fixated, receiving enough hand clapping support to stay where she is. (2) When they clap too little, the student will "regress" back to the place where she last received sufficient hand clapping support. (3) When class members are inconsistent with their applause, the student will become confused about what is expected of her. (4) At times the class will see that their hand clapping supports more than one behavior at a time. For example, they might applaud when the student is walking in the right direction, but at the same time singing a song; one behavior is desired, the other superfluous (or worse, in real life, maladaptive).

Stop the exercise when the student reaches the final goal or is stuck. Either of these contingencies should occur within five minutes. Sometimes the student just stands at the door too long. If she has not spontaneously started to move in a minute or so, suggest that she try walking.

Lead a discussion about what happened, relating what happened in the exercise to what happens to clients. The potential lessons to be learned are: (1) When approximations are too hard for clients to understand, they will fail to meet their goals. (2) When clients receive too much support for reaching an intermediate goal, they will tend to get stuck, having little motivation to move on to the next step. (3) When clients receive too little support for reaching a new approximation, they will tend to regress to an earlier behavior pattern where they received adequate support. (4) Sometimes support for one behavior can also support superfluous or maladaptive behavior if it occurs with both patterns.

4. Ethical issues of assessment

Present to your class the following scenario: You are working in a mental health agency. A client comes in to see you for case management services. She has many serious family problems, including a degree of depression that seems to be "situational," based on the current problems she is facing. Clearly, she needs help, and she reports that she cannot afford private counseling. You work for the only mental health agency in the town. Your agency charges client fees on a sliding scale. Your client is not eligible for Medicaid, but has health insurance through her employer. She cannot afford to pay, even at the bottom of the sliding scale fee schedule. After informing her insurance company of her situation, you find out that the only way they will reimburse your agency is if she has a mental health problem that is severe enough to be given a "dysthymic" or "major depression" diagnosis from the DSM-IV-TR. (Explain to your students, if necessary, what the DSM-IV-TR is and that some diagnostic codes will allow at least some reimbursement from health insurance companies and some won't.) Your colleagues tell you that even though the client does not have a serious enough depression problem to be diagnosed with one of the two DSM-IV-TR codes that would allow her to pay for your services, you should diagnose her with one of these depression codes so that she and her family can receive your help. She is in desperate need of help from your agency and will not receive it unless your agency receives reimbursement from her insurance company.

Ask your students to form small groups of four or five to discuss the legal and ethical implications of this course of action and report back to the class. Follow up the group reports with a class discussion. You might wish to inform the students that applying DSM-IV-TR codes in marginal situations to allow agencies to receive reimbursement for services is a common practice.

7 Additional Components of Case Management Intervention and Evaluation

Intervention in case management is the act of putting into practice the components of the service plan that has emerged from assessment. It requires that case managers master many generic roles and skills applicable in different organizational and community contexts. As you may remember, these include direct support, crisis intervention, short-term counseling, making referrals, advocacy, and central coordination. Other special skills are also particularly important for case management: contracting, negotiating, record keeping, and evaluation.

Contracting

The ability to contract is important for case managers in dealing with clients, with colleagues, and with anyone else in the community who might be of help in their work. In business, a contract describes the obligations of each party in the performance of an agreement. People make less formal contracts all the time. An agreement between father and son to go to the movies if the boy cleans his room is a contract. So is an arrangement whereby a wife will cook and her husband will do the dishes, or one will shop for food and the other will clean the house. Although most of these contracts are made orally, some are written down so that there will be no confusion about who agreed to what.

A case management contract in social services is similar to other social contracts. It is an agreement between a worker and a client that the client will perform some behavior. The worker may also explicitly promise to do something, but this part of the contract may be implied rather than stated. As in other situations, most of these contracts are made orally, although some are put in writing. Examples: A client agrees to arrive on time for his appointments; the worker agrees to be there to provide a service. A client agrees to attend AA meetings; the worker shows positive support, implying that he is pleased. A client agrees not to attempt suicide for the next week (a "no-suicide contract"); the worker agrees that hospitalization will be avoided for the coming week.

There are four components of a good contract between a worker and client: client involvement; behavioral specificity in goal setting; consequences for compliance; and a specified time frame. First, it is always best if the client is part of the contract decision-making process. People don't like to be told what to do. Of course there are times when workers have to dictate a client's behavior, but they should avoid doing so whenever possible. Involvement in the contracting process is more than a question of values and self-determination. Experience and research have shown that when people actively participate in deciding what is best for them, they are more likely to do what they promised.

Second, the agreed-upon behavior expected from the client should be explicit. This is the contracted goal. A lack of clarity about expectations is probably the most common factor when contracts fail. Thus an agreement for a father to praise his son when the boy finishes his homework is not clear enough. The contract should specify clearly how, when, and where the father would do this, and what exactly constitutes a completed homework assignment. A contract with a mother to visit her daughter in foster care every Saturday is sufficient only if the worker assumes that the mother knows what to do with her daughter once she gets there; a better contract would specify what the two will do during the visit. A contract for a client to attend a day treatment program three times in the next week lacks clarity; a better one would state what time he will show up, how long he will stay, whom he will connect with, and what he will do while he is there.

The third component of a good contract involves the consequences for compliance and noncompliance, usually for the client but sometimes for the worker as well. Too often social contracts omit this crucial step. (It is never omitted in legal contracts.) A good contract always makes clear a meaningful positive consequence for compliance; it may also specify a negative consequence. Whether or not a worker and client discuss the consequence for contract compliance, it is always implied. At the very least, workers imply that they will be pleased if clients perform as agreed, and sad, disappointed, or annoyed if they don't. This type of consequence may not be sufficient to support people in performing behavior that is difficult for them, but we should not underestimate the value of worker praise for compliance, especially when a good professional relationship exists. We can always hope that there will be something positively intrinsic in the contracted activity, such as feeling good about oneself, having fun, or accomplishing something that draws praise from significant others. Sometimes workers have to find temporary "artificial" positive supports, such as access to special activities, or even arrange for tangible rewards.

Negative consequences, which may be indicated for noncompliance, usually involve threats: hospitalization, loss of benefits, placing children in foster care, losing visitation privileges, or prison. Using threats as the major way to motivate behavior is not a good learning model—it simply doesn't work well. However, the threat of negative consequences is often a natural part of social behavior, so when they are not obvious, they should be made explicit. We should not assume, however, that the avoidance of a negative consequence is the same as a positive support. By staying sober, a client will obviously avoid many health and social problems, but the absence of these problems is probably not a functionally positive consequence of going to AA meetings. If the avoidance of negative consequences actually worked to change behavior, people would have no trouble in stopping to overeat, smoke, or use drugs. Such is obviously not the case.

Whether positive or negative consequences will turn out to be supportive cannot always be predicted. But workers and clients should proceed with their best judgment and see what happens.

The fourth component of a good social contract is making the time frame clear—the time when it is agreed that the goal will be reached. When is compliance supposed to occur? In other words, when is the contract supposed to be completed? As with the other components of good contracts, simply clarifying the time frame assures that there will be no confusion in this regard.

Contracts fail for the same reasons that clients fail in their attempts to reach short-term goals. The agreements are too hard for clients; clients lack enough internal and social support to motivate them; support is not forthcoming with enough intensity and immediacy; the contract is confusing; promised consequences are not delivered.

Case managers do not make contracts only with clients. On behalf of their clients, they contract for services with colleagues, social service agencies, community organizations, and other people in the community. Every time an agency agrees on the phone to take a referral from you, it is an oral contract. When you find a new community resource for your clients, you agree on how referrals will be made; this too is a contract. So is your agreement to follow up on a client after termination. In all these instances, contracts embody the same principles as those behind contracts with clients. Workers need to be clear about what is expected of all parties to an agreement, the consequences for compliance and noncompliance, and the time frame of the agreement.

Contracts will also be part of your life as a case manager within the organization where you work. The original agreement to hire you is a contract. Making contracts is a common professional activity in supervisory relationships. And administrators frequently request agreements from their staff. Your ability to form satisfactory contractual relationships with the people you work with will be positively correlated with your professional success as a case manager.

Like so many other case management skills, making appropriate and effective contracts takes practice. One cautionary note should be added here. Contracts should be developed only in areas in which the agency/worker has both the intent and capacity to deliver. Unrealistic contracts that cannot be fulfilled leave case managers and their employers exposed or vulnerable to allegations that they have been negligent in their responsibilities because of acts of omission (Gelman, 1992).

Negotiation

Negotiation is a useful tool in all walks of life. It is a set of skills that supports the making of agreements between people in any relationship that involves sharing material, emotional, economic, or supportive resources. As a case manager, you will need the help of many other people and organizations, and you will often have to negotiate an agreement with them to render aid, especially when it is not freely forthcoming. If the sister of a chronic mentally ill client is reluctant to visit her once a week, you may be able to negotiate visits. Again if an agency initially refuses to accept one of your clients, negotiation may open doors for you.

The best kind of agreement to emerge from the negotiation process is one in which each party feels that it has achieved something important and satisfactory. Business dealings do not always reach this goal. In the professional social service value system, however, equity and social justice are very important, so case managers must always strive for negotiation tactics that result in fair and equitable agreements. At the end of negotiations, it is optimal when all parties feel like winners. This is not always possible, but it is a goal for which to strive.

Clearly, many of the skills we have discussed are important in negotiating—active listening, restating, reframing, summarizing, partializing, goal setting, and contracting. Negotiating also calls for the additional skills of assessing needs, setting boundaries, making offers, maximizing similarities while minimizing differences, taking a stand, polarizing, power plays, co-optation, and compromising.

Negotiations begin with knowing what you want and *assessing the needs* of the other party. If you negotiate without knowing what you want, you are essentially asking the other party to determine your needs for you. You will then define your position by reacting to what is presented to you, which puts you at a disadvantage. In addition, having some idea of the other party's position before you negotiate helps you to set your *negotiation boundary*. This is your bottom line—how much you will and won't accept. By setting your bottom line before discussions start, you will know when you reach a situation where you need to walk away instead of settling for an unsatisfactory agreement. In the best negotiations, each side *makes an offer*, a statement about what it wants. It may include what a party is willing to do or give in order to get what is desired. Different strategies come into play here. Some people ask for much more than what they want, expecting to reduce their demands later. Others ask for exactly what they want. Still others make it clear they are asking for less than what they want with the expectation that this tactic will help them later. ("You owe me one.") Part of making an offer is obviously tactical, but it also depends on your negotiating style.

In difficult negotiations, one of the most helpful skills is to *maximize similarities and minimize differences*. When participants seem to be at an impasse, focusing on where they are in agreement is an excellent tactic to get discussions moving again. *Taking a stand* is another tactic that can further negotiations at strategic points. It involves stating a hard-line position—but is often used in conjunction with a concession. "My geriatric client has to be enrolled in your day treatment program all day—but I can agree to find a volunteer to work there with him four hours a day." *Polarizing* can also help move negotiations along by articulating clearly the differences between parties and focusing on how much each side has to lose if an agreement is not reached. Polarizing may clarify essentials that have been lost in the heat of difficult discussions, but it is a potentially risky strategy and should be used with caution. The *power play* is another problematic strategy. One side threatens to pull out of the negotiation if it doesn't get its way. The power play is best used when negotiators have some acknowledged base of power in the relationship. Labor unions resort to a power play when they go on strike. During the civil rights movement of the 1960s, protesters threatened to close down bus systems, restaurants, and universities by nonviolent tactics that were essentially power plays. When it works, this strategy ends up with people returning to the negotiating table.

Co-optation is a strategy in which one side tries to win over a negotiating adversary by means other than the negotiation issues. You can do this in many ways: by developing a friendship with the other party; by offering other supports so that your adversary will be more open to your position; by providing opponents with the opportunity to put themselves in your shoes so they will see the value of giving in to you. Constructive examples of co-optation can be seen when black and white adversaries live in each others' communities for a period of time; when public officials who make policy for the poor are given the opportunity to work with welfare recipients; or when labor officials arrange for industry executives to work on the assembly line. It is hoped that co-optation of this sort will make negotiations more equitable. There are times when co-optation can be viewed as unconstructive or even unethical. If people feel that the co-optation is a veiled attempt at manipulation, negotiations will be much more difficult. (Bribery is, of course, an unethical and illegal co-optation tactic.)

Almost every negotiation involves *the art of compromise.* We use the term "art" advisedly, for compromise requires an understanding of human nature, the intuitive ability to size up people, and a good deal of horse-trading sense. Every good negotiator understands that people need to feel that the deal they are making has something in it for them. Being able to work out such a deal in a seemingly impossible situation demands considerable creativity. In recent years, international agreements on arms control have met with success, while negotiations to achieve peace in the Middle East show just how difficult compromise can be.

One of the most common impediments to successful negotiation is the need to save face. Saving face is a pervasive dynamic in all human interactions, an issue in relations between parents and children, between partners, between generations, and even between nations. Case managers will see the dynamic with all of their clients, particularly with those who are mandated for service by the courts. The person who can help people save face when making compromises —be it in a family, in a therapy session, with other agency personnel, or between nations—will be viewed as a powerful negotiator.

Record Keeping

Record-keeping systems in social services in general, and in case management programs in particular, are a challenge. The goal is to have a place where all the important information about a client is carefully documented. This would include the psychosocial, assessment information, diagnosis, medication records, intervention records, goal attainment data, and termination summaries. The challenge is to develop a recording system that allows the case manager to document this information as efficiently as possible. The record-keeping rule of thumb should be this: Whatever data you record about your clients should be useful to you or have value to other professionals. In some cases, you will need to keep specific information solely for its potential use in legal proceedings.

Case management record-keeping systems face five potentially serious problems for workers and administrators: (1) controlling the time it takes to put information into client records; (2) making client data meaningful and reasonably available to the worker; (3) making pertinent data in client records readily available to agency personnel for program evaluation; (4) being able to efficiently transfer pertinent client information to other community professionals; and (5) complying with new HIPAA requirements. The first problem, the time spent in record keeping, is the bane of every case manager. We all understand that records have to be kept, but every minute we record is a minute that we could have been working on behalf of our clients. Balancing these two needs is no easy task, especially when you feel that what you are being asked to record is unnecessary or will rarely be used. To make matters worse, professional program evaluators reviewing client records find unusable sheet after sheet of information, much of it written in longhand and barely readable, if readable at all. Even if information is typed, it is often so voluminous as to make information retrieval impractical and/or costly.

Data accessibility is also of paramount importance. Process or outcome information that you or your supervisor cannot easily access is a waste of worker record-keeping time. Difficulties in documenting client progress and goal attainment make supervision less meaningful and the transfer of records to other agencies extremely troublesome. Workers end up putting in significant recording time and then more time in trying to find needed information. Agency administrators are periodically asked to summarize client demographics and to document the progress and outcomes of the total client population. Specific information in each client record thus needs to be transferred to an aggregate data pool describing whom the agency is serving and how well they are being served. It can be very time-consuming to access this essential information unless there is an efficient record-keeping system. These issues now have to be addressed within a new framework that requires agencies to have written policies on the collection and dissemination of protected health information and to provide training for workers on issues of privacy and consent procedures.

There are no easy answers to these problems, but recent innovations in record keeping offer some promise. For example, Goal Oriented Record Keeping (GORK) systems and Problem Oriented Record Keeping (PORK) systems make the dreaded narrative progress report an efficient notation that combines goal attainment data with a very short note about significant client contacts and agency contacts on behalf of clients. These systems allow for quick and easy assessment of worker inputs and client progress, which can be used by case managers to efficiently track their caseload, to help in supervision, and for overall program evaluation. These new types of client records do not mean that case managers can completely avoid the psycho-social and progress notes, but they do make the process more meaningful and efficient.

Many agencies have developed checklist formats to take the place of part of the psycho-social narrative. This type of record can be helpful for both workers and administrators. Some agencies are able to enter worker and client information in computer systems to facilitate record keeping. There are also programs that allow workers to enter data in their own laptops for later transfer to a central agency computer. And some systems use "scan sheet" technology, which allows psycho-social and progress note data to be directly scanned into computer spreadsheet and statistical programs. Remember, all computerized record-keeping systems must comport with HIPAA regulations regarding protected health information.

No matter how efficient record keeping becomes, however, you will need to sharpen your writing skills and your ability to interpret the meaning of what you find in client records. This is especially important for client records that have become voluminous over time. Your records will be judged by how well you keep your notations up to date, whether all required forms are in the file, and, yes, by how neat and orderly it is. Those of you whose writing is illegible, who tended to procrastinate on your homework assignments as students, or had messy rooms as children, may need to clean up your act in the client record-keeping department. The client record is not a novel, but a working tool that documents worker inputs, indicates client progress and outcome, and provides the basis for client and program evaluation (Gelman, 1991, 1992).

Evaluation of Case Management Practice

The reason most people work in social services or health services is that they want to help others. The most natural question you will ask with every client you see is, "Was I helpful?" This is not always an easy question to answer. First, you must have some idea of the goals to be accomplished. It is impossible to evaluate practice without goals. But even with them, evaluation is difficult. When your clients fail to meet their goals, it is very hard to assess how much of their failure was your responsibility. The reverse is also true: when clients do well, it is not always clear how much is due to your work with them. However, we wouldn't be in this business unless we believed that case management can help people meet their needs, and that clients can do better in life when they are connected to helpful, caring people and services. Thus the major practice evaluation question, whether clients succeed or fail, is: How much can you attribute their outcomes to your work?

Three major case management outcome factors explain why clients fail. First, the case manager's lack of skills may be at fault. Second, people have a hard time changing their lives if they do

not receive adequate support from significant others, community networks, or other institutions. Such is the case when family members, friends, or neighbors refuse to help; when economic support from the government is insufficient; or when
community agencies fail to provide adequate service. Third,
clients may have psychological or biological characteristics that
make it very hard to be successful. Such is the case with addictions, chronic mental illness, serious illness or disabilities, and
a history of serious abuse.

The outcome of every case depends on all three of these factors, so that assigning responsibility for client outcomes becomes
a complex interaction among them. Regardless of how clients
fare, however, most workers can learn something about their
case management effectiveness and efficiency by evaluating
their own practice (For suggested research directions, see Yarmo,
1998). Case management *effectiveness* has to do with how many
clients attain goals as compared with the larger group of similar
clients in a particular agency or in the population as a whole.
Thus, if all other case management outcome factors were equal,
and this is rarely the case, the worker whose clients had most
successfully attained their goals would be considered the most
effective. Case management *efficiency* has to do with how much
professional effort and time are required for a group of clients to
reach their goals. Let us assume that two workers have the same
types of clients and that all of them are about equally successful
in reaching similar goals. If one worker could achieve this end
by putting in half the time required by the other, the first worker
would be considered more efficient. Effectiveness and efficiency
are not necessarily correlated. A very efficient worker might
manage a large caseload, seeing each client only a few times, but
have a poor record of client success. Conversely, a worker with
a caseload of only ten families could be very effective, but, by
spending too much time on each case, would not be efficient.

Even though assessing effectiveness and efficiency is obviously affected by all three case management outcome factors,
self-evaluating your effectiveness and efficiency will always
help you. If you judge that your clients are not as successful as

you would wish and neither their personal characteristics nor community factors seem to be at fault, you should assess your own skills. How are your "connecting skills"? Are you missing important areas during assessment? Does your goal setting lack clarity? Are you tracking clients frequently enough? Have you found the best referral sources in your community? Do you need to be more proactive in resource development? Are your advocacy skills adequate for the situations your clients have encountered? Are your negotiation and contracting skills satisfactory for the tasks at hand? Do you need to address an administrative or supervisory problem in your agency that is hindering client care?

Another way to gauge your effectiveness and efficiency is to compare your practice with that of your colleagues. This process can produce competitive tensions, but can be a wonderful learning experience when done in a supportive collegial atmosphere. Each of you has skills and ideas useful to the others. Workers with more years in the field have obviously developed skills that can help their less experienced counterparts. In this context, however, it is unfair to judge each other's practice, since so many case management factors affect client outcome. The only reliable way to compare case managers is to assign clients randomly so that no one worker ends up with more difficult clients than any other. Since random assignment occurs only in the context of research projects, comparisons in everyday practice are not necessarily meaningful. If a group of workers and/or their supervisors understand this fact, they can learn much from sharing their experiences with each other.

The second factor to evaluate when clients in a case management program are less than successful is their personal and organizational support system. No matter how skillful the workers, it will be very difficult to attain and maintain goals if clients' personal support systems are seriously inadequate. Most people cannot change their behavior or maintain desired changes unless they get support from people who care about them. No amount of case management, therapy, community programs, economic support, or cursory volunteer or professional contacts will change this basic fact. If you judge that this is a major problem for a client, your work will be cut out for you. You will have to help organizational and community support systems find better ways to connect more personally with your client.

Another point for you to keep in mind is that it is quite common for clients who do well in intensive case management programs to regress after they are handed over to a community support system. No matter how good a job you do, your clients are dependent over time on the quality and accessibility of the health, social service, and social support resources in their community. If these resources are poor or not easily available, don't expect your clients to have a satisfactory long-term success rate. You will suspect this when you notice that clients in one referral agency are doing poorly compared to those in other similar agencies.

The third outcome factor contributing to client failure is the one you probably have the least power to affect—the client's personal history and characteristics. It is well known that certain problem areas, among them alcohol and drug addiction, chronic mental illness, poverty, and chronic ill health, are fraught with difficulty for clients and case managers. High rates of recidivism are to be expected here. For example, clients addicted to cocaine face a strong biochemical addiction aside from all the other psychological, social, health, and community factors affecting them. Clients with severe physical disabilities face inherent personal challenges regardless of the quality of resources available to them. All you can do in such cases is try to bring all of the interpersonal, social service, health, and economic resources you can to each situation. Sometimes research produces innovations that can ameliorate these clients' conditions—new psychotropic drugs, improved prostheses, or better treatments for chronic diseases. When this happens, we should expect to see dramatic change in case management programs, such as what we have already seen with the advent of breakthrough treatments for AIDS.

While it is clear that some problems are harder to deal with than others, inherent difficulties should not be seen as the only reason for high rates of recidivism. Improvements in professional skill levels, streamlined agency structures, increased economic support for families and the agencies that serve them, and broadened community resources should go a long way in helping clients better meet their needs and achieve goals that are important to them and to the communities in which they live.

For the Teacher or Trainer
Optional Exercises for Chapter 7
1. Contracting

Ask students to pair up and choose roles. Instruct the student worker to make a contract with the student client. You may choose what the contract issue should be, depending on the focus of the case management training. Common contract issues are ongoing attendance for a service; keeping an appointment; "homework" assignments for practicing a new behavior or exploring potential family/community resources; taking medications; staying abstinent; or refraining from performing some behavior. The worker and client should come up with an explicit written contract for the coming week which has all of the following components: (1) behavioral specificity for the behavior under contract—the contract goal; (2) the client's responsibilities in performing this behavior—who is involved, when it will occur, and where; (3) the worker's responsibility as a support; (4) the positive consequence for compliance, (4) (optional) the negative consequence for noncompliance; and (5) the time frame. After the contract has been formulated and written down to the satisfaction of both the worker and client, they should both sign it.

It usually takes from fifteen to twenty minutes to complete this exercise. If there is time, the students should switch roles and do it again.

After the exercise is completed, lead a discussion about the process of making a contract based on students' experience in this exercise. Ask for some students to share their contracts and discuss them with the group.

2. Negotiation

Many negotiation skills can be practiced in role-plays, but some are harder to simulate than others. What is important in developing negotiation role-plays is to have a clear scenario around which to practice skills in both the client and organizational domains. This scenario should include the background of the situation, what is at stake, and, in organizational settings, the bases of power and structural relationships of those involved. Case management is performed in so many different settings that it is difficult to develop a satisfactory generic situation. The best scenarios for negotiation role-plays should be developed by the teacher/trainer either alone or working with the class/training group.

Once the parameters of the role-play situation have been clarified and the focus of the negotiation made clear, students can practice several different skills. Note that discussion precedes skill practice.

Negotiation boundaries: Lead a discussion to clarify what a worker might want from a negotiation. Ask students to discuss their bases of power as they enter the negotiation; these would differ depending on whether they are negotiating with a client or with a supervisor. They should then decide what is the least they could accept (their bottom line), and what would be their optimal outcome.

Making an offer: Ask students to discuss what the opening offer should be and, in terms of strategy, who should make the first offer, whether the worker or the other party (client or supervisor).

Taking a stand: Have students discuss the conditions under which they would take a stand—that is, make an offer that would appear to be nonnegotiable. (Some students should actually verbalize how they would do this in practice.) Emphasize that this is a strategy; it can be done with tact and does not necessarily polarize negotiations.

Maximizing similarities and minimizing differences: Have the students imagine what the significant differences could be as the negotiation develops. Ask them to verbalize how they would clarify these during the negotiation, with the aim of satisfactorily resolving the issues where there is similarity before dealing with differences.

Compromising: Ask students to think about positions they might be willing to modify in order to gain more of what they want. Discuss what saving-face issues might impede a compromise.

The role-play: There are two ways to conduct this negotiation role-play. In one, have students pair off, one playing the worker and the other the client or supervisor. Then have short scenarios of two to five minutes, in which each student has a chance to play each party in one of the negotiation components discussed above. Then, either between themselves or with the larger group, they should talk over what happened.

The other way is to have students form triads, with the third student acting as an observer, noting on paper each time the worker uses one of the negotiation skills. Then stage a role-play of fifteen to twenty minutes, in which the student worker will have a chance to practice all of the negotiation skills listed above, in an attempt to complete the negotiation. After each scenario, the triad would discuss what happened, using the observer's notes as a guide. In this model, each student should play each role, so that it would probably take about an hour for completion.

3. The Thread Negotiation Exercise

One of the most important problems to resolve in negotiations is to find a way that all parties can save face and end up feeling like winners. An interesting way to simulate these dynamics is the thread exercise. Get a regular spool of thread, any color, and a piece of chalk. Ask the students to pair up. Each set of partners should find a space where they can face each other about five feet apart. Give each dyad a five-foot piece of thread. Then have someone go around the room and draw a line with the chalk about halfway in-between them.

Tell the group that each pair will be having a tug-of-war, not with a rope but with the thread. Let them know that *there must be a winner.* To win, one player pulls his partner over the line without breaking the thread. If the thread is broken during the tug-of-war, both lose. If they break the thread, you give them one more piece to try again. If they ask any more questions about these instructions, just repeat what you have said.

The actual exercise takes about five minutes. When it is finished, discuss what happened and relate it to what happens in real negotiations. One issue is easy to relate to real life. Many negotiations are so delicate that pulling too hard breaks them down, as when the thread breaks if partners in this exercise pull too hard and break their thread. Also discuss what it means to be a winner and to save face, and how it relates to what happened in this exercise. There is a satisfactory resolution to this exercise, and some students may figure it out. Discuss how they did it.

4. Ethical implications of evaluation

Present this scenario to your class: Your agency is being visited by a "site visit" team from one of the major funders of your drug and alcohol program. The agency director has asked the staff go through the agency records and document the treatment outcomes for the clients over the last year. It turns out that out of one hundred clients in the last year, sixty, or 60 percent, dropped out within four weeks of entering treatment; out of the other 40 clients, only 20 percent of them, 8 clients, successfully reach their treatment goals; the other 32 clients reached some of their goals before leaving treatment but did not gain abstinence. Your director has two ways of reporting these statistics to the site visit team. She can say that the agency had a 20 percent success rate, if one views only those clients who stayed with the program for more than a month, or she can report that the agency had an 8 percent success rate, if one looks at all clients who entered treatment in the last year. The director chooses to report to the site visit team that the agency had a 20 percent success rate for the year.

Ask the class, either in small groups or in a class discussion, to take sides on this issue and explain why. You might also mention at some point that a 20 percent success rate for drug and alcohol treatment is considered to be the average success rate in this country. The question is, on what basis is this rate calculated?

5. Cultural implications of negotiation

Explain to the class that the ability to successfully negotiate, either professionally or personally, involves the ability to assert oneself. These assertiveness skills need to be performed strategically in a negotiation and include the ability to say no, the ability to express anger constructively, the ability to express what you will and will not tolerate in someone else's behavior, and the ability to make requests and demands. There are many ethnic, cultural, and religious groups in Americain which women in marriages and families are expected to be submissive to their husbands and other male family members. These groups include religious Christians, religious Jews, Muslims, Hindus, and some Hispanic, Asian, and Middle Eastern cultures. Ask the students to form small groups and describe to one another what they were taught about women's roles within marriage and the family and whether culture or religion was part of this socialization. Then ask them to discuss the implications of training women to be more assertive and to negotiate more effectively in marriages or families where the women have traditionally been more submissive. You and your students may have some personal experiences with this dynamic to share with one another during a subsequent class discussion.

Part 3
Case Management Populations and Problems

8 Case Management Issues with Special Populations

The case management method is basically generic regardless of where you work. Case managers go about their business determining eligibility, conducting comprehensive psycho-socials, doing assessment, setting goals, intervening in a wide range of personal, organizational, and community targets, and tracking client outcomes. However, certain client groups and problem areas may require certain specific focuses. Often it is obvious how various client groups shape the work of case management professionals, but sometimes the issues are more subtle. At the very least, workers have to be sensitive to the special needs that different client groups bring to the case management milieu. It is not possible to cover all of these special populations in this volume. Social service and health professionals work with so many people and problem areas that it would take a treatise of encyclopedic proportions to make sure that nothing was missed. The overview that follows will discuss some of the major special groups.

Developmental Disabilities

Developmental disabilities is the current diagnostic term covering such problems as mental retardation, autism, learning disorders, and attention deficit-hyperactivity disorders (ADHD) (American Association on Mental Retardation, 1992). Many case management programs deal with clients suffering from one of these problem areas, usually focusing on either children or adults (Baerwald, 1983; Feine & Taylor, 1991; Gelman, 1974, 1983, 1989; Hanley & Parkinson, 1994; Horejsi, 1979; Seltzer, Litchfield, Kapust, & Mayer, 1992; Simmons, Ivry, & Seltzer, 1985; Wehmeyer

& Metzler, 1995). All of these diagnoses present special and at times difficult case management challenges. The difficulty is proportional to the severity of the disability and whether the disability is viewed as temporary or lifelong.

When working with these clients the most important first step, if it hasn't already been taken, is to make sure that the client has been appropriately diagnosed. Stories abound of how children and adults have been diagnosed as mentally retarded when they actually were learning disabled, or how a child diagnosed with an emotional disorder was really autistic. Often children who are viewed as disruptive in class end up with an ADHD diagnosis; sometimes these problems are better seen as reflecting difficulties in child management. Case managers may not be trained to make these diagnoses, but they certainly should know where to refer clients and their families for evaluation and assessment. An accurate diagnosis will suggest how severe the developmental disability is and whether the family is looking at short-term interventions or a need for lifelong support.

Guidelines for case management/service coordination with developmentally disabled individuals were adopted by the American Association on Mental Retardation (AAMR) in 1994. These principles are consistent with NASW's 1992 standards on case management, which were presented earlier. (AAMR suggests that the term "service coordination" is more respectful than "case management" and advocates its use.) The ten-point statement is as follows:

1. Service coordination (case management) is an ongoing process that consists of assessment of the wants and needs, planning, locating and acquiring supports and services, and monitoring or follow-along. The individual and/or family is the defining force of the service coordination process.

2. Service coordination is an essential coordinating service that should be made available to all persons with mental retardation/developmental disabilities who need and/or request it.

3. Service coordinators are responsible for locating supports and services to enable people to meet their goals. Generic systems and natural supports should be utilized prior to using segregated services. Full inclusion in society requires that people receiving service coordination are provided the support necessary to access other systems.

4. Service coordination must be a flexible service and the extent of the service provided should reflect the needs and desires of the individual and family. It is an ongoing relationship which should increase or decrease in intensity as needed and requested by the individual and family.

5. Advocacy is an integral component of the service coordination process. Advocacy is done both on an individual basis and may be extended to a system wide level to benefit the common good. In every manner possible, the service coordinator provides support to individuals and families to advocate on their own behalf.

6. Service coordinators should document their work in ways that record the individual's preferences, dreams and aspirations, and the progress and barriers to accomplishing these goals.

7. Throughout the service coordination process, the service coordinator should provide education to individuals and/or their families. This education should promote their effective involvement with this process on their own behalf so that people can effectively participate in, and ultimately, independently coordinate their own services. This promotes the opportunity to terminate their involvement with service coordination at some point if they choose.

8. Service coordination agencies have an obligation to share the information about desired and needed supports and services with the appropriate service delivery system to ensure a system that is current and responsive to people's needs.

9. The number of individuals each service coordinator works with will need to be kept to a minimum in order to ensure the service coordinator the opportunity to establish strong working relationships with individuals and families. In addition, resources need to be sufficient to allow for appropriate supervision and administrative support of service coordinators and for purchase of service for people receiving service coordination.

10. Service coordination agencies should be autonomous from direct care providers of services and administrations which fund services, to ensure that service coordinators receive complete support to act based on the preferences and needs of the individual rather than the needs or constraints of the agency. In addition, individuals should be able to select their own service coordinator. (AAMR 1994)

These provisions are designed to provide services to "clients with complex, severe, long term (and often life long) needs that affect many, if not all, aspects of their lives and cut across service delivery systems" (Baerwald, 1983).

Case management for children with developmental disabilities is different from case management with adults. Most of the children referred for these problems have some primary family members with whom they are living—parents, grandparents, or other relatives. Therefore, the "client" needs to be viewed as the entire family, not just the child. Parents caring for children with serious mental retardation, autism, or learning disabilities will need considerable support. Not only are they concerned about getting the best treatment for their child, but they often face frightening economic consequences for this treatment, especially if the disability will be lasting. Strains can affect the marriage and relationships between siblings and other family members. In addition, families need help in negotiating the complex social service, health, and welfare systems to access the services they need for their child and themselves as the years go on.

A good example of what case managers face with children's developmental disabilities can be seen in the case of an autistic child. To diagnose autism requires well-trained and experienced professionals. A child can seem normal for the first year or two of life and then begin to show markedly abnormal behavior, such as withdrawal and retarded development in the areas of speech, motor behavior, and cognitive and social skills. Autism can look like retardation, mental illness, or just slow development. Its prognosis is unpredictable, but apparently if a child is unable to communicate by the age of five or six, he or she will probably need extensive social service support for life. In some cases, children have been "cured" and are able to attend public school and lead a relatively normal life; in other cases, children will never achieve independence and will thus need lifetime support.

Once an autistic diagnosis is made, case management goals for the family become clearer. The child will need intensive early treatment, with goals aiming for a modicum of speech or signing skills, motor skills, and social skills by the time he or she is ready for grade school. The parents will need training in how to deal with the child's behavior, which is often explosive and un-predictable, and how to support academic and social skill learn-ing at home. Family therapy may be required because the strain on families with autistic children is severe and family relation-ships are definitely at risk. Parents have to deal constantly with a child who can be sweet and gentle one minute and violent and destructive the next; other children can become jealous of the time and energy devoted to the autistic child. Another big prob-lem is economic. The cost for adequately treating autistic chil-dren is very high, running up to $50,000 a year. Parents need help obtaining the public funds available to support treatment. And maintaining parental employment is a critical issue, linked as it often is to health-care benefits. Losing a job becomes a fam-ily crisis of mammoth proportions. While all these issues exist in a two-parent family, one can imagine how they are magnified in single-parent households.

Some developmental disabilities can be dealt with on a short-term basis. For example, ADHD can often be treated successfully in a short period of time either through teaching parents and teachers behavior modification child management skills or through medication for the child. In these cases, the focus of case management can include finding intensive training for the child's parents or caretaker; arranging for teachers to receive in-service training in classroom management procedures; finding appropriate school placement; and referring the child to a physician or psychiatrist for medication.

When case managers work with adults who have developmental disabilities, they face different problems. Many retarded citizens, diagnosed long ago, have few remaining family support systems. Their parents may have died or may be too old to be burdened with their care and upkeep (Seltzer, Wyngaarden Krauss, & Janicki, 1996). Essentially, the welfare system becomes responsible for their lives. The immediate goal for their case management is to assure them adequate housing, food, health care, and economic support to take care of basic needs. An important assessment task is to ascertain their ability to live independently, and the need for life-skills training (Schalock, 1996). Some clients will be able to work and live independently and thus require minimal social service support; others will need twenty-four-hour supervision. Once clients are placed in adequate living arrangements, they may need other supports, such as day treatment, life-skills training, job training, supported employment, health care, and access to welfare benefits.

When there are family members who are willing to help a disabled relative, case managers have additional options. These might range from finding enough support for the family so that the client can live with it to arranging for visits as frequently as advisable. Some families have cared for their now adult mentally retarded family member since he or she was a child. But as parents get older and/or lose economic resources, this may become impractical. They may want to continue caring for their family member, but will need to be connected with additional community resources in order to do so. Or it may become clear to the case manager that even the most well-intentioned family members cannot continue in their caretaking role and will need help in allowing other community resources to take over (Seltzer et al., 1996).

To summarize, the case management of children with developmental disabilities needs to include their parents or caretakers as the client. A competent diagnosis should be an immediate focus, with referrals for intensive treatment for the child and support for the parents as the direct result. With adult clients, case managers should immediately assess family supports and quickly address food, housing, and supervision needs.

Health Care and Chronic Illness

Case management in health care settings is a common role. Social workers, nurses, and other health professionals work with patients and their families during hospital stays, arranging for what they will need once patients go home. The focus of this work depends on whether recovery is likely or the illness is chronic (Berger, 2002; Berkowitz, Halfon, & Klee, 1992; Cesta & Tahan, 2003; Cohen & Deback, 1999; Loomis, 1988).

For example, when patients successfully undergo heart bypass surgery or are recovering from an accident, there is every reason to believe that they will get well. They and their families need to know how to make recovery more successful. They may need to be linked with community agencies to help in this process, such as local rehabilitation facilities, short-term support groups, economic resources to tide them over until they can work again, and transportation. Case managers thus play a teaching role. In addition, with the advent of managed health care, paying for expensive medical treatment can be extremely complicated, and many clients will need help in negotiating the maze of regulations and applications to keep them from financial catastrophe (Perloff, 1996).

When an illness is diagnosed as chronic, the case management process is different. Families immediately face the shock of the diagnosis and what it may mean to their lives. Crisis intervention is a common case management method in these cases. Such crises occur at different levels—emotional, financial, and educational. The patient will need help in understanding the implications of the diagnosis, the course the disease will take, and the treatment options available. He or she will need plenty of emotional support as well. The family, too, will be worried about the patient and the effects the disease will have on their lives. Chronic illness can be an economic disaster for a family, so an additional case management focus will be to explore how to pay for long-term treatment. During the course of this work, the case manager will need to be a source of information in order to inform the patient and family about all of these issues. Case managers need not be experts in particular diseases, although many workers do develop such expertise. They do, however, need to know where to help families obtain information. When illnesses are chronic, families need various forms of long-term support. Not only does the family require economic stability, but the patient and family will be under increasing emotional strain as time goes on. Diseases that have unpredictable outcomes, such as cancer and AIDS, and those that slowly cause patients to lose the ability to function, such as multiple sclerosis and lupus, keep patients and their families in progressive states of anxiety, having constantly to adjust to new realities as the disease follows its course. Referrals for support groups and continual access to individual and family counseling thus become essential. With chronic illness, it is important for case managers periodically to connect with clients over long periods of time.

The current state of health care in the United States poses an additional challenge to case managers. The complexity of the healthcare system, with constantly changing federal and state Medicaid and Medicare regulations, managed care requirements, and increasingly complicated outpatient and hospital administrative procedures, requires that case managers become advocates for their patient clients and families. Advocacy in hospitals, with their hierarchical structure of doctors and administrators, can create especially challenging conditions. Case managers may determine that the needs of the patient or family are in conflict with the hospital's policy or physician's practice. These situations require excellent co-optation and negotiation skills because case managers exist toward the lower end of the decision-making professional totem pole. Similarly, working through the morass of managed care rules, combined with hospital and physician policies, can tax the time and skills of the most ardent case manager. Yet this kind of advocacy is becoming an important part of the role of workers in health care settings.

To summarize, case managers who work in health care need

to attend to patient support in a family context where possible. They need to develop crisis intervention skills, and be able to provide basic information about the course of diseases and the types of support that will be needed. In addition, they have to become experts in the economics of health care and act as advocates for their clients in the health care system.

Mental Health and Chronic Mental Illness

People enter the mental health system for many reasons. Some exhibit the "normal" difficulties of living expressed in the "V-codes" in the DSM-IV-TR, such as marital problems and parent-child conflicts. Others suffer from very severe mental illnesses, such as schizophrenia or chronic depression. It is possible to find case management programs in every type of mental-health facility, but they are more common in settings that deal with serious mental illnesses (Biegel, Tracy, & Corvo, 1994; Edinburg & Cottler, 1990; Kanter, 1989, 1991; Moxley, 2002; Rapp, 2002; Shera, 1996) and may focus on what Moxley (2002) describes as recovery-based case management. Individuals, couples, or families that are dealing with more "normal" interpersonal difficulties or relatively minor personal problems often go directly to clinical social workers, psychologists, psychiatrists, or psychiatric nurses for short-term therapy. If case management is done with these clients, these clinical workers may integrate it into the therapeutic experience. However, since personal and family problems interact with almost every issue case management programs deal with, referrals for mental health services are very common.

Whenever a case manager suspects a more serious mental illness, it is essential that qualified mental-health professionals evaluate the client and provide a DSM-IV-TR diagnosis. Once such a diagnosis is established, it should dictate treatment options. If the case manager is not a part of a mental-health program, it is usually a good idea to transfer the client to a case management system that is accustomed to working with such clients (Lamb, 1980). It might be possible for two case management programs to coordinate with each other. There is no reason, for example, why case managers working in a child-welfare system cannot coordinate their broader intervention efforts with workers in a psychiatric mental-health program.

The focus of mental-health case management differs depending on whether the primary client is a child, an adolescent, or an emancipated adult (Belcher, 1993; Bond et al., 1988; Borland, McRae, & Lycan, 1989; Bush et al., 1990; Itagliata, 1982; Johnson & Rubin, 1983; Rubin, 1992; Werrbach, 2002). With younger clients, the case manager should involve the parents or caretakers when possible (Marcendo & Smith, 1992; Scannapieco & Hegar, 1994). It is extremely difficult to help children and adolescents who have serious emotional problems if their parents or parental figures are not directly involved the treatment process, not least because the latter are often under considerable stress themselves. Coping with serious childhood and adolescent mental-health problems—disruptive behavior, violence, obsessive-compulsive disorders, or depression, sometimes accompanied by suicidal ideation or actual suicide attempts—is an enormous burden for parents. They need support, not only in helping the patient but also in dealing with their own feelings. Thus referrals for family as well as individual therapy should always be considered as part of case management intervention when young people are involved. In addition, as with any family in a crisis, parents may face economic, health, housing, and child-care problems that contribute to their child's illness and hinder their ability to deal with it. Typically, therefore, the case management of families with mentally disturbed young people will require referrals for more than therapy.

If young people are deemed out of parental control or a serious danger to themselves or others, they may have to be hospitalized or placed in foster care. A case manager may be the professional coordinating these placements, offering support to both the family and the other workers or acting as a mediator between inpatient facilities, foster care, and family members. The skills of the case manager in coordinating, brokering, and mediating are critical in such cases.

Adult clients who suffer from chronic mental illness offer a different challenge to case management (Rapp, 2002; Rapp & Chamberlain, 1985). Like adults with developmental disabilities, they require assessment as to the feasibility of family support. Thousands of people with psychiatric disorders are homeless in this country, and many of them are also addicted to drugs or alcohol (Rife, First, Greenlee, Miller, & Feichter, 1991). Housing and basic living needs are always an issue when working with this population. Next in order of importance is locating help when medications are called for. It is not enough to insure that adults with serious mental disorders have their prescriptions filled; many need continuing support and monitoring in taking them as well. Sometimes the difference between living independently and institutionalization depends on medication. Once housing, food, welfare benefits, and psychiatric care are established, many other services have to be considered, among them therapy, day treatment, family counseling when indicated, job training, education, and socialization programs.

To summarize, the case management of children with serious mental health problems should include their families whenever possible (Litwak, 1985). Good diagnosis is critical, since it directs a wide range of child and family supports. When hospitalization or foster care is indicated, the case manager needs to take on a coordinating, brokering and/or mediating role. Adults with chronic mental health problems may need help with housing, food, and basic health care. They often require additional support and monitoring when medications are prescribed.

Addictions

Drug addiction in this country (and around the world) is at epidemic proportions. Legalized drugs include cigarettes, alcohol, and prescription drugs; illegal drugs include marijuana, heroin, crack, cocaine, and a wide variety of so-called "designer drugs." Some people also view overeating and obesity as addictive behaviors. It doesn't necessarily matter to the client or to society whether a person's drug of choice is legal, the effect on her or his life and on the community can be devastating. Cigarettes are associated with many diseases, economically draining both families and society; obesity is correlated with morbidity. Alcohol addiction is widespread, affecting work, family stability, automobile safety, and causing personal tragedies among all economic, racial, and ethnic groups. The effect and impact of illegal drugs on communities and families is also well documented.

A significant number of case managers work with addicted clients, whether in hospital drug and alcohol (D&A) inpatient and outpatient programs, specialized drug or alcohol centers, or in mental-health services (Hall, Carswell, Walsh, Huber, & Jampoler, 2002; National Association of Social Workers, 1993; Siegal & Rapp, 1996, 1997; Sullivan et al., 1994). Theories explaining addiction view it variously as a disease, as a lifestyle, as a habit, and as a biochemical interaction. Each of these theories, or some combinations of theories, dictate different focuses of treatment, but all addiction treatment modalities center on group support. Almost all alcohol and drug programs refer clients to Alcoholics Anonymous (AA) or Narcotics Anonymous (NA), respectively. These twelve-step programs are run by those in recovery—that is by the clients themselves, with no direct professional involvement. Related to AA are similar groups for those whose lives have been affected: Al-Anon for the partners of alcoholics; Al-Ateen for adolescents; and Al-Coa, for the adult children of alcoholics. Once an addictive diagnosis is made, a referral to one of these groups is mandatory in most case management programs.

Assessing whether a client has an addiction is not an easy task. Many people who are addicted to alcohol or drugs are unaware of the problem or do not acknowledge it. Many can function for years before the addiction begins to affect their lifestyle, health, and families. Case managers in every social service and health agency should be trained to recognize the signs of possible addiction. For example, many adults drink periodically, getting drunk only on weekends. These "binge drinkers" can carry on this way for years without knowing they are addicted. Unfortunately, such behavior is usually progressive, and often ends up with debilitating health, employment, and family problems that can destroy careers and families.

Diagnosing addiction is only a first step for case managers. A common characteristic of alcoholics and drug addicts—at least those who have not "bottomed out" and become seriously debilitated—is denial. Family members may also deny that a young person or a partner is addicted. Thus one of the first steps for the case manager may be to convince an individual or family that addiction exists. In this situation, the case manager functions as a teacher, an essential role in the case management of addictions (Sullivan, 2002; Sullivan, Wolk, & Hartmann, 1992).

Obviously, addicted clients must be referred for treatment, and, as previously mentioned, eventually to AA, NA, or similar self-help programs. For the seriously addicted, hospitalization may be necessary so that they have help during the withdrawal process. Complete withdrawal from drugs or alcohol is an important treatment goal, but it can be extremely difficult, posing potential psychological and health risks. There are many inpatient facilities equipped to help people withdraw from alcohol or drugs. Case managers need to know where these settings are, what they cost, how they are financed, and how to get people into them. Once withdrawal is completed, recovering addicts need intensive support from their families, friends, and, possibly, employers. Case managers often arrange for this support through referrals for therapy, group help, and specialized employment programs.

As scientists learn more about the biochemistry of addictions, there will be more options available to help people battle their addictions. One option is the use of another drug, methadone, as a non-debilitating alternative to heroin. Case managers working in methadone clinics perform similar tasks as those working in other addiction areas. However, they have an additional role—coordinating the dispensing of methadone, and making sure that clients take it as indicated. As time goes on, there will likely be more such drugs that either act as alternatives or inhibit the effects of addictive drugs.

It is very important to realize that family members must be involved in the long-term treatment of addicts if at all possible. Non-addicted family members need to change their behavior as the client works to change his or hers. Family behavior that serves to perpetuate or encourage addiction is known as "code-pendency" or "collusion." Family members need to separate themselves from dysfunctional ways of dealing with a recovering addict. Case managers, therefore, may have to find support for all members of a family if needed, including spouses, other partners, adolescents, and children. There are even programs for preschool and school-age children in families with a recovering parent. As we have seen in other areas, clients in addictions treatment may need other services as well. While the drug may be the paramount controlling influence in maintaining an addiction, other psychological and environmental factors must often be considered. Chronic depression and anxiety are often correlated with addictions; so are poverty and joblessness. Poor health usually accompanies long-term addiction. Case managers have their work cut out for them in assessing the factors that have contributed to an addiction and managing as broad a scope of interventions as possible.

A unique case management responsibility in working with addictions is that of designing community support systems for long-term drug-free behavior and then tracking clients over extended periods of time. Recidivism in drug treatment programs is high. One should never underestimate the power of drugs over people who have once been addicted. Cigarettes and alcohol are freely available everywhere, with advertising to keep us constantly exposed. Drinking is part of the American lifestyle, with alcohol an integral part of social gatherings in families, at parties, and in restaurants. To maintain sobriety in such settings can be a herculean task. While illegal drugs are not as freely available, people usually return to communities where they are easy to obtain. It is no wonder that so many people fall off the wagon, even after being abstinent for long periods of time. The challenge in the successful treatment of addictions is to find ways to help people not only to become abstinent but to remain so for life.

The role of case management in this long-term process is essential, and it may be that case managers are the only professional group in the field of addictions treatment who are trained for this complex task. They must understand that referrals to programs offering short-term support are only the first step in a successful recovery. The next step is to connect addicted clients and their families to those services that will help stabilize new lifestyles. Many different addiction "triggers" can re-emerge as life goes on. People need to have an immediate place and person with whom to connect as stress builds up, or they will fall back into old patterns. Unfortunately, this long-term support is too often left up to the clients themselves or to community agencies that are not equipped or committed to follow clients after recovery begins. Recovery is a lifelong process for addicted clients; it is a real challenge to the professional community working with them to make lifelong support part of a coherent treatment strategy.

Child Welfare

The child welfare system is one of the most common settings using case managers (New York City Task Force on Managed Care in Child Welfare, 1996). The term "child welfare" is a generic one, and can include any and all services involving a child's well-being, whether the focus is on mental illness, developmental disabilities, economic aid, child protection, adoption, or child support in divorce situations. The one thing that should be clear in child-welfare case management, whether its focus is community based, strength based, or integrated, is that the primary client is always the child (Mather & Hull, 2002). It is the responsibility of the case manager to assess the child's physical and emotional condition, the appropriateness of his or her living arrangements, treatment by the adults and siblings with whom the child lives, and whether he or she is at risk. This goal is the same when working with children no matter how they enter a social service or health system, but clearly, child-welfare agencies have the well-being of children as their major focus.

Protective services are a critical aspect of child-welfare agencies. Situations in which a child may be the subject of physical, emotional, or sexual abuse or be in danger of neglect or abandonment require timely and effective intervention. Once such referrals are received, it is the primary responsibility of the case manager to quickly assess the validity of abuse allegations. This is sometimes difficult, as adults do not readily admit to being abusers. Therefore, case managers working in these situations need comprehensive training on how to assess and investigate allegations of abuse, especially when the signs are not obvious.

The stakes are very high in these assessments. First and foremost, the safety of children may be at risk, and there may not be much time to make accurate and complete determinations. Also, however, the rights of parents must be protected from unfair or distorted allegations. Case managers in protective services have the awesome responsibility of determining from their assessment whether children should be allowed to stay with their parents. This is a task that cannot be undertaken lightly and must be done with care.

The ability of case managers to determine the validity of abuse allegations is complicated by excessively large caseloads, the need to make case findings quickly, and the necessity of documenting their work each step of the way. Then, if the results of these assessments indicate abuse, they must determine the degree of its severity and suggest an immediate remedy. At this point, their work is coordinated with the judicial system, as only a judge can order that children be placed out of the home or force parents to accept and participate in services in order to keep their children at home.

To complicate matters further, child-welfare case managers have to function as coordinators and mediators between parents, social service agencies, and the courts. When children are at risk, so are the parents. Most child-welfare programs try to help parents care for their children at home. They have to guide them to services that specialize in alternatives to foster care for children at risk. Parents who have abused their children need counseling. If parents have neglected children, the reasons for this neglect must be assessed and appropriate parenting and economic services obtained. Abuse and neglect are typically associated with drug and alcohol addiction and with poverty. If these conditions exist, case management interventions will be directed to appropriate help for parents.

It is also the case manager's responsibility to track and monitor how well parents are reaching service and treatment goals, and to determine whether they are ready to take care of their children. If a child is in foster care, a case manager must recommend that he or she be returned home (Stein, Gambrill, & Wiltse, 1977). If a child has already been returned home from foster care or has remained at home under close supervision, a determination needs to be made stating that parents are ready to go it on their own. This is the termination phase in child-welfare case management. However, even with terminated cases, case managers may still have to track families to ensure that children remain in a safe environment.

Case managers have several options in protective service cases, depending on the specific situation and the availability of child welfare interventions, which vary from state to state. If in-home supported services are not appropriate or feasible, the next option is placing the child in foster care. Each state has developed a system of foster-care arrangements in which children can be placed on either a temporary or a long-term basis. In some settings, the child-welfare case manager who refers the case to foster care is also the one who coordinates the placement. In other cases, there is a separate case management system to monitor and support foster-care parents, biological parents, and the children. In any case, such placements are an emotional shock to both children and their parents, and referrals for mental health services should always be considered. Case managers act as mediators between the courts, foster-care homes, other social services, and the child's parents or guardians. Co-optation, negotiation, and personal connecting skills are important as workers face conflicting needs and mandates.

Increasingly, case management programs in child welfare favor keeping children at home while closely monitoring parents (Marcendo & Smith, 1992; Werrbach, 1994). Family Preservation programs, for example, place a case manager into the home for up to twenty hours per week, working with parents, siblings, relatives, and children at risk. Case managers in Family Preservation are trained in a wide variety of direct and outreach skills. They train parents in child management skills, deal with crises, conduct short-term family and individual therapy, and personally connect children and adults to needed community social services (Allen, 1991). The goal of this kind of intensive work is to avoid placing children into foster care. There are many other child-welfare case management programs that attempt to achieve this same goal by referring and coordinating social services; community agencies are expected to provide the intense support that will keep children in the home.

Some parents or relatives are deemed unable to care for a child. In these cases, case managers have to provide long-term foster care or arrange for adoption. Both of these options can present problems. There is a good deal of instability in most foster-care systems. Unfortunately, many children are placed in a succession of foster homes over time. This happens for many reasons. Foster parents may decide to stop taking in children. Some foster children have serious emotional problems and need more skilled parenting than foster parents possess. Financial reimbursement may be insufficient. Some foster parents may be unsuitable because of their own personal problems. Adoption is also difficult, as there are simply not enough adoptive parents to go around. The process is complicated by the advanced age of many of the children, by their special needs, and by legal roadblocks.

Case managers in child welfare face very difficult challenges, but certainly no job is more important than helping children at risk, with the potential of making their homes safe places in which to grow up. Case managers need to become adept in assessment and tracking skills, and be effective in their coordinating, mediating, and referral roles.

Geriatrics

In the late twentieth century and certainly well into the twenty-first century, an increasing percentage of aging Americans will need case management services. Many of the elderly barely subsist at poverty levels, living alone with little to no support. Many more have health conditions that require home-care services such as meal preparation, supportive care in nursing homes, or intensive skilled nursing care on a twenty-four-hour basis. And many can benefit from day programs at senior centers that offer activities and opportunities for socializing.

Case management has become an essential professional service in all of these geriatric situations (Austin, 1993; Austin & McClelland, 2002; Quinn, 1993; Sullivan & Fisher, 1994). Senior citizens enter the social service network from various points. An elderly person who needs help might be identified by neighbors, a welfare worker, family members, doctors, mental health centers, family centers, private practitioners, hospital staff, or homeless shelters. To complicate matters, services for seniors are often disconnected or uncoordinated. For example, low-income families that can no longer care for an aged family member face what often seems a void of services. Long waiting lists for supported housing or nursing-home care are legendary. Finding affordable home care, as an alternative to institutional placement, is extremely difficult. Seniors who live on their own and are increasingly unable to care for themselves often do not know where to turn for help and lack the necessary energy to wade through the social service and health network.

Case managers specializing in working with the elderly can be found in many different settings, sometimes as part of specialized geriatric programs (Eggert, Friedman, & Zimmer, 1990; Kane & Caplan, 1992; Moore, 1987; Morrow-Howell, 1992; Nelson, 1982; Soares & Rose, 1994). These specialized programs can be associated with hospitals, mental-health centers, family-service agencies, senior centers, supported housing, or nursing-care facilities. There is even a growing group of social work and nurse practitioners who work privately as case managers to help families find the help they need to support aging family members.

Case managers working with senior citizens must be active advocates for their clients, as well as having a working knowledge of economic, medical, and housing entitlements for low-income aged clients. Each community has different resources for its aging population and their families, so case managers need to understand the economic and eligibility requirements in their service areas. Basic medical, psychological, nutritional, and housing needs are always the foundation for case management with the aged. Other areas to consider include opportunities for socialization, mental-health support, addictions services, and, when possible, better connection with family members. When seniors live with family members, or when other relatives or friends might help, case managers need to assess their needs if they are to be a continual support for the aging client.

In the coming years, an increasing number of professional

case managers will be working in geriatrics. It is probably a good idea for all case managers to learn more about the dynamics of health care and social services for the aged. Most families who connect with a case management program will eventually be dealing with problems associated with aging family members: the need for placement; diminished cognitive functioning; medical needs; and ultimately, issues related to dying.

Criminal Justice

Case management in the criminal justice system covers a wide range of situations. It starts with programs for youth at risk or in trouble, continues with programs that are alternatives to incarceration (including services for those on probation), and follows with support for clients who have completed jail terms and/or are on parole. Specialized programs in the criminal justice system help the addicted, the mentally ill, those with a combination of mental health and addiction problems (the MICA—mentally ill, chemically addicted), perpetrators of abuse, violent criminals, and juvenile delinquents (Frankel, White, Walzer, Lamon, & McAuliffe,1998).

Case managers who work with populations whose "client career" is involved with the courts or prisons deal with unique conditions. For example, a MICA client could be treated in the community, in a mental-health center, in a drug treatment center, or in jail if he has been arrested for buying or selling drugs. As you can imagine, the dynamics of treatment would be quite different for both clients and case managers in these three situations. In corrections, case managers must understand how the court system works and familiarize themselves with a wide range of issues: arrest; pretrial hearings; clients' legal rights; the meaning and types of criminal charges; the roles of prosecution attorneys, defense lawyers, and judges; access to Legal Aid; probation; different types of incarceration; and parole. For example, the focus of case management may depend on whether the charge was a felony or misdemeanor and on what options the judge has given the client. If the charge is a misdemeanor, the judge might allow the client to be assessed for an alternative-to-incarceration program. If the client has been convicted of a violent crime and sentenced, the judge might suggest that the case management team work with the parole department to determine if there is an appropriate community placement and when the client might be ready for it.

Along with tracking clients through the criminal justice system, case managers also conduct assessments, collect psychosocial information, and make hypotheses about why clients became involved with the law. (Causative factors might be seen variously as poverty, drug addiction, poor housing, lack of employment opportunities, family dynamics, or mental illness; each of these issues, solely or in combination, would direct case management interventions.) Of particular importance is tracking clients after their involvement with the criminal justice system has been terminated. Recidivism in the court system is a serious problem, with some clients being seen again and again over the years (Cote, 2003; Siegal, Li, & Rapp, 2002).

Recidivism involves a general breakdown in a community support system that is unable to help clients make significant and lasting lifestyle changes (Solomon & Draine, 1995). To be more specific, people backslide when they become homeless, stop taking their psychotropic medications, become re-addicted to drugs, lose their jobs, or face family problems. It is of paramount importance to develop community and agency support systems that will stay connected with such clients long after they have terminated from case management programs connected with the criminal justice system. Tracking and long-term maintenance are among the critical challenges facing case managers involved in these systems.

HIV/AIDS

Since the mid-1980s, case management has been the method of choice for organizing and delivering services to those afflicted with HIV/AIDS. (Emlet & Gusz, 1998). The case management method and the skills of case managers fit well with the multi-problem and multisystem needs of those afflicted with HIV/AIDS (NASW, 1992). The integrated service model advocated by NASW is both client centered and culturally responsive to the unique needs of this diverse population. Case managers assist and facilitate in the mobilization of resources to manage both the disease and the environmental stressors that often leave those with HIV/AIDS feeling overwhelmed and powerless (Chernesky & Grube, 1999, 2000; Giddens, Ka'opia, & Tomaszewski, 2003; Thompson, 1998). The particular skills of case managers in systems advocacy and service coordination are critical in ensuring access to services for this population that is often stigmatized and subject to discrimination, particularly in the areas of housing and employment. Given the nature and fluidity of symptoms, living with HIV/AIDS poses both psychosocial and spiritual challenges that vary over time as the disease progresses or goes into temporary remission. The availability of new treatments increases options for the client but makes new demands on case managers.

Chernesky and Grube (1999) identify six types of activities that case managers employ in working with those experiencing the ravages of HIV/AIDS:

- helping clients manage their health;
- helping clients obtain and maintain essential entitlements;
- helping clients obtain essential services;
- helping clients develop skills in activities of living, including communications, negotiation, and self advocacy;
- helping clients develop a support system; and
- helping clients increase their level of self-esteem and in turn their overall quality of life.

These activities involve interventions, both direct and outreach, at the micro, mezzo, and macro levels, with and on behalf of clients (Frankel & LaPorte, 1998). A unique aspect of the case management process with this population is the need to address the emotional and service requirements of the children of clients who may be becoming increasingly more incapacitated. Or, the children themselves may be infected and/or alone following the death of their parent(s). Of special concern when working with this population, and especially with children afflicted with HIV/AIDS, is the emotional stress and burnout experienced by case managers. Strug and Podell (2002) point out that when infected children on managers' caseloads get sick and die, the case managers' self-esteem and their sense of the meaningfulness of their work are weakened. Providing support for these case managers is critical to their ability to continue to function effectively. (See also Grossman & Silverstein, 1993; Liou, 1997; Schoen, 1998; Wade & Simon, 1993.)

Case managers need to engage clients in an educational process addressing prevention and risk reduction. Concerns over privacy and confidentiality may be more critical for this population than for any of the other vulnerable populations served by case managers.

The Homeless

Perhaps no population group is as difficult to case manage as the homeless. This group includes men and women of all ages, including a surprising number of runaway adolescents and families with young children. They are hard to find; they often avoid professional help; they have multiple areas of need; and once enrolled in a case management program, they are hard to sustain in services and have a high recidivism rate.

The problems the homeless face on a daily basis are enormous. First, of course, they have no place to live. In the warm weather, their beds are park benches, sidewalks, and abandoned buildings. In cold weather, they sleep wherever they can to keep warm at nights, sometimes coming into homeless shelters during the coldest nights. The homeless are common in urban centers, often seen sleeping on the street or in parks wrapped in blankets or newspapers, sometimes accompanied by a shopping cart full of all their worldly possessions. Not having a place to live is not just a question of comfort. Being homeless subjects people to serious health risks resulting from exposure to inclement weather and the lack of basic sanitation—there are no baths or toilets on the street. In addition, their physical safety is at risk, as they are vulnerable to street crime and molestation (Heslin et al., 2003).

In many cities, most of the people who live on the street are addicted to drugs. At best, they are forced to panhandle to support their habits; at worst, they must resort to petty crime, such as shoplifting, purse snatching, or burglary. Compounding their addictions, many of the homeless have chronic mental illnesses, ranging from severe depression or anxiety to more serious and debilitating mental illnesses, such as manic depression or schizophrenia. When people are addicted to a drug or to alcohol and also suffering from a chronic mental illness, they have a "dual diagnosis," also described as having "co-occurring disorders" or as being mentally ill-chemically addicted (MICA).

Making the case management of the homeless even more difficult, the treatment of co-occurring disorders needs a much more comprehensive treatment regimen, both for therapy and for medication, than drug treatment or the treatment of chronic mental illnesses alone. People need to be treated for their addiction at the same time as they are treated for their mental illness, which sometimes requires case managers to coordinate these services between two different agencies. In recent years, there has been significant progress in developing concurrent drug and mental health treatment for co-occurring disorders at the same treatment site. However, these treatment strategies require significant motivation from the client for anywhere from six months to more than a year and sometimes require that the clients live in a treatment facility for part of that time. Thus, a homeless person would have to have a high degree of commitment to leaving the streets in order to benefit from these programs. Furthermore, these programs are very expensive, and there are always more people wanting these services than what are available, so finding a "slot" is often difficult, even for a motivated homeless client (DeLeon, 2000).

Beyond all of these issues, the homeless face significant problems in the areas of economic support, nutrition, basic health services, job training, education, and employment. In addition, many homeless have contracted HIV, either through unprotected sex or the shared use of needles, making their health needs even more critical. Clearly, the homeless population needs the entire gamut of what the case management process offers. Because they are usually not at the office door asking for services, the question is how to connect them with a case management process.

Case managers around the country have attempted to connect with the homeless in a number of ways. The homeless congregate at homeless shelters, particularly in cold weather. When they enter a homeless shelter, they are fed and given a place to sleep. During the time they are there, case managers have the opportunity to visit with them and offer their services. In these initial encounters, it is critical for the case manager to use all of his or her engagement skills. Forming a trusting and caring relationship is central to bringing a homeless person or family into a case management process.

In some case management programs for the homeless, case mangers actually spend most of their time on the streets, going to the places that the homeless congregate during the day. They first attempt to connect with them informally. If they are able to form an ongoing relationship, they offer to help when it seems appropriate, slowly trying to draw the person or family into formal case management.

Another place to connect with the homeless is in city jail systems. In New York City, for example, it is not uncommon for the homeless to stay on the streets during the warm months and then commit some petty crime before it gets cold so that they can be arrested and put into the city jail system during the winter. While in jail, they receive some treatment for their drug addiction and/or chronic mental illness. During this time, case managers can connect with these men and women, forming relationships with them before they are released and arranging for housing, drug and mental health treatment, economic support, and other needs prior to their release. This type of program has worked very well in New York City (Frankel, 1999; LaPorte & Frankel, 2000).

While case management with the homeless is challenging, it is important work. In the larger cities, it is impossible to ignore the problem. In smaller American cities, and even in rural areas, the homeless are sometime more hidden from public view—but they are there, and they have the same needs as the homeless living in large urban areas.

For the Teacher or Trainer
Optional Exercises for Chapter 8
1. Personal experiences with the helping profession
    Each of your students has probably experienced, either personally or with relatives or friends, some of the problem areas for case management discussed in this chapter. If your class has

a self-disclosure confidentiality contract, or is willing to make one, ask them to share their experiences with the helping profession for one or more of these problem areas. This can be done in small groups, in a class discussion, or in one- or two-page papers to be handed in. If short papers are chosen, you can tell students to put their names on a cover sheet, which after being handed into you, will be torn off to ensure confidentiality. You may then share the stories with the class as a whole or hand them out randomly for students to read and report to the class for discussion. Focus on the strengths of the helping process, as well as the frustrations and impediments, described in these stories that are representative of the challenges for case management.

2. Agency or personal interview concerning client populations

Ask students to choose one of the case management areas discussed in this chapter and then visit an agency that deals with this issue in order to interview an administrator or staff member. (Another option is to ask the students to interview someone in their family or one of their friends.) You might consider asking the class to decide together, based on their readings and class experience, what questions they should ask during the interviews so that there is some uniformity. If there are too few agencies, have students go in teams of two or three for these interviews.

9 Challenges and Visions

As we move further into the twenty-first century, the practice of case management will need to evolve. Fiscal restraints resulting from ever shifting local and national political priorities, of America's changing ethnic and cultural influences, advances in medical and social service technologies, and the changing demographics of the population will all challenge case managers and their ability to provide effective service to clients. It is not possible, of course, to predict the future, but it is possible to determine with some degree of accuracy what problems case management will need to address in the short term to maintain and improve services, and to identify potential problems that could impair the effectiveness of case managers in the long term. In addition, there is evidence of positive trends upon which case management can build into the future.

Challenges: Overcoming the Sisyphus Complex

There are a number of challenges now facing case management that will dictate the future quality of services and the definition of the field itself. These include training, accreditation, reputation, caseload size, dosage, staff turnover, and cost-containment or provider-driven policies vs. client-driven organizational policies. Most are not insurmountable, even when they seem to be. Sometimes case management practice in the social and medical service professions can seem bleak, especially in the face of too many clients, too few successes, and organizational dynamics and social policies that are often difficult to negotiate. Despite this, one of the first and most important tasks for a case manager is to lend a positive vision to the client, offering hope in what are seemingly hopeless situations. It is similarly important for case managers to view their own profession in the same way. After all, why do people enter the helping professions unless they believe that positive change is possible, even in the most difficult circumstances?

Training, Accreditation, and Reputation

One of the most promising trends for case management is the continual upgrading of training for practitioners. Many students in accredited schools of social work offering bachelor's of social work (B.S.W.) and master's of social work (M.S.W.) degrees receive some training in case management in the context of social and medical service organizations. Similarly, students who specialize in nursing, or in one of the associate degrees related to the medical profession, are either required to have case management training or are given the opportunity to complete course work and gain practical experience in the field. The National Organization of Case Managers membership is growing, and it is now possible to earn a case management accreditation certificate through the National Academy of Certified Case Managers. That's the good news for attempts to improve the practice of case management through training.

The bad news is that the settings for case management are extremely diverse. While this phenomenon shows the broad need for the field, it results in too little agreement as to what should constitute actual practice, who should be called a case manager, and whether there can be a convergence to generic practice models and a body of knowledge that can support some type of standardized accreditation. Accreditation should be suited to the many types of case managers found in the social and medical service professions *and* be supported by the organizations that employ them.

Protecting the professional reputation of those working in the field of case management continues to be a challenge. One still hears of workers outside the field, such as those employed by managed care companies who approve and track medical payments for patients, being referred to as case managers. In some settings, where true case managers have been overwhelmed with cases, or where local resources for clients are scarce to nonexistent, the title has been associated with poor service or even worse problems. There have been situations in which the negative associations with the term *case manager* have been so great that the title has been changed to some other term, such as *care coordinator*, even though the actual practice is still case management. Clearly, case managers, and the people who are educating them, need to be concerned with who is allowed to be called a case manager and what they are expected to do.

Given these issues, it is important for case managers to join their respective professional associations and lobby for a more standardized national accreditation credential and for clearer definitions about who should be called a case manager. There is sufficient precedent in this country for this endeavor. For example, child care workers specializing in early childhood education and drug and alcohol counselors both have a national accreditation process separate from standard college degree programs. Case managers deserve no less.

Caseloads

Another challenge that will affect case management in the future is caseload size. There is, unfortunately, too little data to suggest an optimal caseload size, particularly because of the many different settings in which case managers work. One could conceptualize settings where a worker-client caseload of 1:50 or 1:100 may be indicated, especially if the problems being resolved are transitory or relatively concrete. Using groupwork techniques, it might be possible to build rather large worker-client ratios and still have comparatively good services and outcomes. It is more likely, however, that lower caseload ratios allowing for frequent and ongoing client contact would be more appropriate. Thus, a decision as to what would be an optimal caseload should take into consideration the number of times per week or month a case manager would need to meet with each client to bring about necessary outcomes.

What actually determines caseload sizes in social service agencies and medical facilities, however, often has more to do with budgetary realities than successful client outcomes. Administrators are dealing with finite and often shrinking sources of funds for case management staff in the face of an increasing need for services. Given this situation, many administrators choose to increase caseloads so that at least a modicum of services can reach all of those in need. Whether this strategy is the best for these organizations or their clients is certainly questionable, one that needs to be documented and compared with client outcomes over time. At best, this strategy forces staff to make difficult decisions; at worst, it causes serious consequences for both the agencies and their clients, as has been seen in recent years in some of the nation's child welfare and foster care agencies.

When caseloads become too large for even minimal case management services, there is no simple solution. The cause can be a decrease in public funding, such as when state or federal governments decrease social service budgets, and/or an increase in the number of clients needing services, as has resulted from the recent Latino immigrations into America. The changes to social policies and public funding resources that are usually part of long-term community organization and political strategies can also create difficulties for social service agencies. Yet there are numerous instances where these long-term strategies have shown promise, with some increases in state and federal services for senior adults and broader funding for Head Start being two cases in point.

One immediate strategy for lowering caseloads in the face of state and federal budgetary constraints is to obtain funds from "soft money" sources, such as foundations, state and federal grants, and local fundraising activities. There are more than seventy thousand philanthropic foundations in this country giving away money to support a wide variety of social service and medical programs. (All of these foundations can be found online through the Foundation Directory, www.fconline.fdncenter.org.) Applying for these funds is not difficult; most of America's foundations have very short, simple applications. Applicants do not need special training in grant writing to complete them.

There are also numerous state and federal grant opportunities that fund social and medical service projects outside of the normal public funding streams. However, the applications for these grants are much more complicated than those for foundation grants, and they do require some degree of training in grants-manship. (All grants available from the federal government are listed in a government publication called the *Federal Register,* which is available at most public libraries, with a limited version available free online at http://www.gpoaccess.gov/fr/.)

Many organizations employing case managers have some soft money supporting their services. There are clear advantages to accessing these types of funds, as they can fund programs when no other funding is available and augment programs that have inadequate funding. However, these types of funds usually cannot be counted on for the long term. "Hard money," or funds coming from city, county, state, and federal legislative sources, is usually more secure. While the available hard money may ebb and flow for a particular problem area or when client populations change, there is usually some money available. Medicare and Medicaid are two examples of hard money sources. Soft money awards from foundations or grants are usually fulfilled over the course of one to five years. Thus, agencies have to worry about the sustainability of programs supported with soft money. Once these grants are fulfilled, staff must secure other sources of funding, either by applying for other grants or by asking local governments to extend their hard money funding to sustain a particular program.

Dosage

Closely connected to the issue of caseload size is the amount of time, or the "dosage," that is required to allow the case management process to work. The term *dosage* comes from the medical field, and more recently from addictions research, to suggest the amount and type of intervention needed to bring about a desired change. Obviously, the number of clients that a case manager has to see per week is related to the amount of time he or she has to perform interventions toward successful goal attainment. As is true for optimal caseload size, there is very little data to suggest optimal dosages because case management is conducted in so many different settings, with such diverse client problems. Very often, the overall number of weeks, months, or years a client stays with an agency is mandated by agency policy, funding sources, or the severity of the client's problems.

It is important that case managers have a clear sense of what is the proper service dosage for the client population they serve and a reasonable hypothesis of the needed dosage for each client specifically. There are some client populations where client contact may be needed for the life of the client, as is the case for many developmental disability, chronic mental or physical illness, and geriatric cases. There are also a number of client problem areas that dictate long-term case management services, such as drug and alcohol treatment and recovery, child welfare, and criminal justice. Short-term case management dosages are more common for the recovery from some illnesses or hospital stays, obtaining concrete entitlements, workfare, immigration assimilation, or other types of problems where it is clear that client goals can be met in a relatively short time.

In the coming years, it will be very important for case managers to support the empirical identification of the optimal dosages for the client populations they serve. This information can be used in many helpful ways. First, it will help agencies establish their financial need with local and federal funding sources concerning their ability to help people. If it is relatively clear that a specific dosage is generally needed for reasonable client outcomes, and the amount of money it will take to provide this dosage is known, then it becomes evident how many clients can be served within given budgetary constraints. This information can have utility in the face of public pressure to resolve community problems. While this may appear to be an optimistic view, it is beginning to occur in the area of addictions, where it is becoming empirically apparent that longer terms of treatment are necessary for desired outcomes.

Second, being able to predict optimal case management dosages will allow workers to suggest the proper number of cases they should be able to handle each week and the number of hours needed for each case. In addition, as more information becomes available on optimal dosages for different client populations, further refinements will suggest how to "triage" cases at intake, so that time frames can be predicted for clients in more difficult situations versus clients that have fewer difficulties or better family/community support systems.

Staff Turnover

Staff turnover is a serious problem in the social and medical services. It is not just a case management issue. It is no secret why most people in the helping professions leave their jobs—too much job stress and too little pay. Those who enter the helping professions do not do it for the money. Yet there comes a point when salaries become an issue, even for the most altruistic and socially committed case manager. After a few years of work, even the most committed professional would change jobs if one with significantly more money was available. Since upward mobility is not an option in many smaller agencies, the only way to improve one's financial lot is to switch jobs. In addition, even as case management positions are becoming more professional, they are all too often viewed as entry-level jobs. Upward mobility is then tied to achieving a college or graduate degree, such as a B.S.W. or an M.S.W., as the ticket for advancement in an agency, sometimes to positions out of the case management area. However, as case management becomes even more firmly established and respected as an essential component in quality social and medical services, salaries and opportunities for advancement should improve in the coming years.

It is not so apparent that job stress in the social and medical services will also improve in the near future. One is constantly finding newspaper and magazine articles reporting how stress is affecting workers in America, and social service, medical, and educational organizations are not immune to these dynamic forces. While the answers to job stress and how it relates to staff turnover are complex, case managers need to address them directly in their agencies with open communication, much in the same way they help client families reduce their stress. It may not be easy, but it is important, not only for staff comfort but also for the benefit of the clients.

One of the essential factors that go into good case management is continuity of care, especially for longer term cases. Since the development and maintenance of a good worker-client relationship is central to case management, staff turnover can play havoc with successful client outcomes. Clients often enter case management services with a history of failed professional relationships, expecting a hard time and little to show for it. Staff turnover forces clients, in a sense, to start over again, not unlike a child who goes from one foster care home to another. The more frequently this happens, the more problematic it becomes for the next worker to establish trust.

Thus, case managers must face the problems of staff turnover not only for themselves but for their clients. There are basically two choices: either resolve the issue so that workers stay in their jobs for significantly longer periods or design intervention models that do not rely so heavily on the worker-client relationship. Both are possible, and the latter will be thoroughly discussed later in this chapter.

Cost-Containment or Provider-Driven Policies vs. Client-Driven Organizational Policies

Many of the challenges to case management practice in the coming decades can be attributed to how organizations conceptualize and institute their case management programs. There are many programs that, either by design or necessity, develop a provider-driven model of case management that is essentially based on cost containment. This model can be seen most clearly in for-profit organizations, including for-profit managed care organizations. In these organizations, providing case management services within a set dollar figure per client, with a cap on the amount of money that can be spent, is most important no matter what the outcome. Even nonprofit organizations are sometimes forced by restricted funding into operating to some degree under a cost-containment model.

What typifies a client-driven case management model is a focus on client needs. This model does not ignore budgetary issues. After all, social and medical service agencies are businesses, and as such, they should be run with an eye to the bottom line. It does clients no good if a helping agency goes bankrupt and closes its doors. However, in an organization that is client driven, the first question asked is, What do the clients need?

Quality of care is foremost on the minds of staff and clients. The agency tries to develop a structure in which good worker-client relationships can be fostered, and clients and their family/community systems are empowered to become involved in their case management planning and interventions. The ultimate goal, when possible, is for clients to become their own case managers. When case managers in these client-driven organizations face budgetary constraints, staff and clients together devise strategies for keeping the quality of care at the highest possible level.

There is a continual dynamic tension in case management programs between budgetary constraints and client care, with the lurking danger that cost-containment and/or for-profit issues will overpower client-driven organizational models. With the advent of managed care, and the push in some quarters toward the privatization of social and medical services in this country, case managers will need to become ever more vigilant.

Visions: Please, Won't You Be My Neighbor?

Four visions for the future of case management are presented below. The first has to do with the development of what is now called an *integrative case management system*. The second has to do with how we conceptualize and label the people with whom we work. The third discusses the case management relationship. And the fourth vision suggests how case management models might be organized to involve and energize the community.

Integrated Case Management

For many years case managers have realized that the effectiveness of their work is partly dependent on the breadth, depth, and quality of community support for their clients. When there are inadequate and/or poor quality services for the client population served by a case management system, the dearth of referral opportunities will make it very difficult for clients to meet their goals. Even when there are good referral opportunities, there still can be many barriers to access for case managers and their clients. Intake procedures can be taxing and laborious; there may be competition between agencies for available services "slots"; after clients referrals are made, the question of who is responsible for overall client services can arise; and case managers may lose track of clients who are subsequently involved with staff from other agencies.

For all of these and many other reasons, case managers around the country have been spontaneously arranging special relationships with those agencies and staff members who are critical to helping their clients meet their service goals. Case managers working with the homeless establish special relationships with staff at housing agencies; those working with clients who suffer from addictions build collaborations with workfare programs; case managers who work with geriatric clients connect with transportation agencies. Many times these types of collaborative relationships are contractual, specifying the number of referral slots available, identifying who will be responsible for ongoing case management, and facilitating application processes.

In recent years, some case management systems have taken this idea even further, developing what George DeLeon, one of the major researchers in this area, has called the *case management integrative model* (2001). In this model, the case management system makes an assessment of what community agencies are essential to the well-being and goal attainment of the client population it serves. The relevant community agencies are then approached to develop informal or formal collaborative agreements to accept appropriate referrals from the case management agency, which generally retains the central case management responsibilities until the client is deemed ready for "graduation." Thus, an integrated, seamless network of community collaborations is established to support clients who enter a case management program. These integrated networks can be quite elaborate, including the entire gamut of services clients need, such as housing, job training, medical and psychological support, parenting training, child services, access to entitlements, legal services, and transportation. This more integrated approach to case management can make for more successful client outcomes, as DeLeon (2000) has reported. This result should not really be surprising. Common sense dictates that an integrated network of collaborating agencies will give better service to clients and will better facilitate professional communication than case management systems that do not have these collaborative arrangements. It is thus likely that the future will bring more of these integrative case management models into fruition, creating more opportunities for case managers to help their clients.

Labeling

Historically, the helping professions have labeled the people whom they are trying to help with a number of terms: patients, clients, members, participants, and consumers. Some of these labels have historical roots; some are the result of an attempt to show that the people in need are part of the helping process; some labels are trying to remove an apparent stigma from those involved in therapy or case management; other labels have their roots in diagnostic assessments. Regardless of how these labels try to define a person who is seeking help, all of them denote a person who has become part of a social or medical service system and as such defines them as seeking help or mandated to seek help. Once that person leaves the system, the label is usually no longer functional.

A systems approach to labeling what have been called clients in this text would use a term that does not simply identify the segment of a community system to which a person has become attached for a time. Additionally, it would not use a term that identifies a person as needing help in some problem area as if he or she were different from other people in his or her community. It would choose a term that could be used across the person's experience and apply to whatever part of the system that person finds him or herself in.

Fred Rogers, the creator and star of the children's television show *Mr. Rogers' Neighborhood,* had a better idea. He started every show with a song that ended, "Please, won't you be my neighbor?" The fact is that the person with a problem that ends up being helped by professionals is not so different from the other people who live in his or her neighborhood, or in your neighborhood for that matter. All people and all families have problems. Some have the financial resources and/or family-friendship networks that allow them to problem solve without involving professionals. Some do not. They are all our neighbors, next door, down the street, with their children in our neighborhood schools. They are working beside us on the job, attending our churches, mosques, and synagogues, sitting next to us at community events. The fact that some have at times faced problems that meant seeking professional help by no means makes these people different from anyone else. Their seeking professional help has just made it more evident that they need help. Perhaps the only difference between those who end up seeking help, voluntarily or by mandate, and those who do not is that one group is more public and the other has managed to keep their problems private.

Of course, there are differences in the types of problems people have and in their severity. But these are assessment and diagnostic issues, not reasons for any special identification based on whether that person or family ended up with professional help. In addition, the fact that society stigmatizes some types of problems, such as addictions, spousal abuse, and felony crime, more than others should not be further compounded by helping organizations. The act of being formally helped by professionals is usually associated with the breakdown of natural neighborhood and community support systems. People who end up needing these alternatives to natural community support do not need to have a label categorizing them as lacking these resources.

There is really no reason to use any special label to designate people who are being helped through social or medical service agencies. If they are truly our neighbors, and they join the organization where we conduct case management services, they are no different than the other people in our neighborhood who seek the services of churches, mosques, synagogues, the YMCA or YWCA, or even the community swimming pool to help deal with some family or individual issue. Most of us are mandated to attend school when we reach age five, and most of us, by necessity, join the workforce when possible. Similarly, some people are mandated to attend, or attend by necessity, social or medical service organizations.

How do we think about people who use their natural community resources, who attend community organizations voluntarily, by mandate, or by necessity? What do we call them? Essentially, we first think of them as members of our community and, on a more local level, as our neighbors. When these community organizations need to identify those who are part of their group, they usually refer to them as members. In the same way, our neighbors who seek help at social service or medical service facilities are also members of these organizations.

If we have to call those seeking help by any particular term, it would seem that members or neighbors would be more appropriate than patients, clients, consumers, participants, or some other label associated with a diagnostic assessment system. For the rest of this chapter, the terms neighbor and member will designate those who are being helped in the case management process. As you see these terms integrated into the following discussions, consider how well they fit with your experiences as a neighbor and a member of community organizations and with what is or will be your professional role in a social service agency or medical organization.

Relationship, Relationship, Relationship

The core of the case management process is the development of a close worker-neighbor relationship. In the same way that "location, location, location" is the mantra for the real estate profession, so should "relationship, relationship, relationship" be the mantra for case management. Any vision for the future of case management should include a more intense focus on building these professional relationships. In fact, there is an emerging database that suggests neighbor satisfaction with case management services is correlated more closely to the nature of the worker-neighbor relationship than it is to people's perception of need or to the actual quality of services delivered. A recent study by Susan Allen (2002) is a case in point. The results of this study clearly show that neighbors attending a case management program in a child welfare agency were highly satisfied with the agency's referrals when they perceived a positive relationship with their case manager, regardless of their perception of the quality of services rendered. In other words, neighbors who felt they had received poor services from the agencies they were referred to still rated their case management experience highly if they liked their case manager.

How can this be? Neighbors simply may be smarter than we think. They understand that it is the close, long-term relationships we have with families and friends that dictate for all of us the quality of our lives and how we weather our family, health, mental health, and economic crises. Neighbors do not blame their families and friends for their inability to receive services from seemingly stupid and unfair insurance or governmental organizations. Nor do they blame families and friends for what happens to them as a result of things that are out of their control, such as economic downturns, health crises, or natural disasters. Neighbors want their family and friends to do the same things we want ours to do: empathize, take our side, fight for our rights and our ability to gain access to resources, and above all, care about what happens to us and stay around when the going gets tough. It is thus not so surprising that when neighbors feel that their case managers are friends who really care about them, they would rate the services highly even if their service goals were not reached.

The moral to this story is that case managers in the future may need to think about their role as being more like that of a neighbor who has special skills to access services and face crises and less like that of a professional who has technical helping skills. This new role requires that case managers be given the time to form and maintain these relationships, meaning that organizational structures and policies must support case managers in creating this important neighbor-to-neighbor dynamic.

The Community Approach: A Model for Case Management in the Future

There are two general assumptions that must be accepted before discussing a community-based case management model. First, the ultimate goal for each member of a case management program is to be empowered to become his or her own case manager, to have a family-friendship network take on this role with or for him or her. Second, all people need to have family and friends in their lives who care about them, who care what happens to them, and who are there both when they need them and when they do not. With these two assumptions in place, case managers must come out of their offices and into the community where members live.

This model also implies that termination from a case management program would be based on far more than symptom reduction and/or satisfactory improvement of quality of life indicators. Successful termination from a case management program would also include (1) a member demonstrating his or her own case management skills over time and (2) family, friends, and neighbors in the member's community demonstrating their ability to perform case management on behalf of their neighbor when needed.

Thus the goal of the community-based model is not just to improve service for case management program members. It is also to improve long-term quality of life for former case management program members, as well as for their families, friends, and neighbors. This approach will also strengthen neighborhoods. With a modicum of professional facilitation and a structure by which neighbors can help one another, this approach can create a cascade effect in which the secretly held problems that most families face can be shared, resulting in even more people helping one another.

This idea is not pie in the sky. There is an innate and untapped spirit of helping within the American people, a spirit that is sometimes forgotten or lies dormant out of disuse. This spirit comes out during disasters especially. No one can forget the outpouring of national helping spirit that came out of 9/11. And whenever there is a natural disaster, such as a flood or a tornado, neighbors are helping one another. This spirit is also apparent in the amazing philanthropy in this country, which comes not just from the rich, but from most of us. We give to United Way, we give to our religious institutions, we demand that our governments give massive amounts of charity through our tax dollars. The helping dynamic in America's neighborhoods is sleeping, awaiting a way to channel its energy. The field of case management, with its theoretical and practical basis in systems theory, is just the catalyst to awaken people's desire to help.

Building the helping capacity of neighborhoods is a good thing for the field of case management, too. Given the ongoing struggles to fund social and medical services with too little money and the always increasing number of people who seek services, there will never be enough case managers to meet the need. Furthermore, a case management program is only as strong as the community and neighborhood support around it. By necessity, case managers rely on organizational, community, family, and neighborhood support for the short- and long-term stability of members. The uncertainties that underlie helping organizations include their ability to

- Track members after termination
- Find other professional organizations that have long-term stability
- Find referral agencies that have quality staff
- Find agencies that do not have a high staff-turnover rate
- Use referral agencies that follow systems theory rather than just taking care of agency-mandated symptom reduction or entitlements
- Avoid agencies that re-refer to other agencies so that members are not moved around like marbles in a Chinese checkers game

Given all of these uncertainties, which exist even in an integrated case management model, case management programs that are interested in providing long-term services have three basic options:

1. "Inoculate" members to become self-reliant in a world that may tend to isolate them, giving them the skills to deal with future problems, including back-sliding.

2. Rely on continuing professional support, with a long line of case managers and other professionals tracking members' needs for years.

3. Rely on family members, friends, neighbors, mentors, and other natural community organizations, such as religious institutions, schools, and the workplace, for ongoing support.

Case managers cannot be put into the position of having to choose between these three options—successful case management will need all of them. However, it is the third option, which utilizes the community, that is most in need of development. The question is, how do case managers go about building and supporting the natural ability of the neighbors in their communities to take care of one another?

First of all, the role of a case manager must be conceptualized as a person who spends a significant amount of time in natural community organizations. Second, case managers must develop assessment tools that show how much support a member receives from family, friends, neighbors, and natural community organizations and start making determinations of what relationships are needed, who is available, and who can potentially be made available. These assessments should be heavily weighted when it comes time for the case manager to determine where to start working to help the program member. Third, case managers should remember that it is the long-term caring relationships that all of us, including the neighbors we work with, need that are associated with a higher quality of life. Termination from a case management program should not be considered unless the member's "long-term caring relationship" indicators show stability.

One of the great advantages of this community model is that families, friends, and neighbors are likely to offer more stable long-term relationships than case managers can. It is this stability of relationships that could greatly improve the quality of life for program members and significantly reduce recidivism.

There are a number of concrete actions that case managers can take to foster the community-based case management model:

1. Ensure that neighbors needing help over time are adequately tracked. For isolated neighbors, it may take a good deal of time to develop a community support system that includes the close, caring relationships that allow for long-term tracking. In order to accomplish this task, given the reality of professional

turnover rates, case managers in an integrated case management model could form teams that would be jointly responsible for program members. One case manager would have primary responsibility for each member. Periodically, the team of case managers could meet with their respective members as a group so that all members would know the entire case management team. If the primary case manager leaves, or if a member is dissatisfied with his or her case manager, then another of the team, whom the member already knows, can take over primary responsibility. This process could only work in the integrated model, as it would require coordination between diverse agencies. However, it is not so different from the process found in what is called a *therapeutic milieu,* where all members of a treatment team meet daily or weekly to discuss members' treatments. One of the barriers to setting up this case management team model, beyond the coordination and time issues, is the lack of a physical location for the integrated agencies. Yet this team approach would ensure some continuity of relationships for members and case managers.

2. Develop a family, friend, and neighbor support system specific to each program member that is monitored and supported over time. Even when program members already have a system of family, friends, and neighbors who are available, these people may need significant support over time. This kind of support is not uncommon for certain types of neighbor problem areas. Agencies helping the developmentally disabled often offer support groups for family members, who are known to need extensive and ongoing support in order to deal with the problems they face. This type of support is also offered for family members who face other types of chronic problems, such as chronic mental and physical illnesses.

Is it really possible to enlist neighbors and friends in these ongoing support endeavors? The answer is yes, if they can be enlisted with sufficient initial professional support. One of the best places to connect with friends and neighbors is through existing community organizations, many of which are used to developing volunteer/mentor services. Volunteer networks are one of the great untapped resources in this country. Many organizations' raison d'etre is to do volunteer work. In addition, all religious institutions offer volunteer opportunities for their members. What is needed is someone, like a professional case manager, to let them know of a neighborhood need and offer the expertise to initially guide and support them. There is no question that some members coming from case management services have difficulties relating to others at times. Therefore, volunteers may need training to learn how to best interact with people who have problems that are unfamiliar to them. It could be a case manager's job to be available to these volunteers for training, for ongoing support, and for connecting members and their families to volunteer/mentors for the types of support appropriate for each situation.

3. Make a concerted effort to build on the utilization of volunteers using a wide range of natural community organizations, including religious institutions, community centers, schools, businesses, and community service groups. What these organizations need is a way to focus their energies, giving people specific programmatic opportunities to be mentors and friends to their neighbors with problems, with appropriate professional support when necessary. Over time, some of these volunteers, many of whom will have had prior experience in social service, education, and medical organizations, may be able to take over some of the responsibilities for the support of their volunteer colleagues.

What is important in the development of a community-based case management model is to make sure that each member who has received case management services ends up with sufficient stable, caring relationships. The people who are part of the member's life sphere should be able to be aware when their neighbor is having a crisis and/or is beginning to slide; when the organizational support system around their neighbor begins to crumble; and when the people support system upon which their neighbor has been depending begins to disappear.

In the coming century, the field of case management could take the lead in empowering and connecting people with their neighbors, acting as the catalyst to help neighbors support one another in their communities, making the American system work for them. We professional case managers need to act more energetically in our attempts to awaken and harness this sleeping community spirit, the same spirit that got us into the helping profession in the first place.

A Case Example

Mike Smith had just received his MSW with a specialization in working with the chronically mentally ill. He returned to his hometown, a medium-sized city in the Midwest, and was hired by a mental health center to coordinate the outpatient treatment of a group of about forty chronically ill people. These program members had recently been released from a mental hospital after spending an average of seven years there. Because of state funding cuts, the mental hospital had been forced to close. All of these program members were over the age of thirty, and most were in their forties. There were twenty-nine men and eleven women. About half of this group were in contact with relatives; some were living with relatives, but most were living in SROs (single-room occupancy housing) or with roommates. All were on some form of entitlement, usually SSI (social security for the disabled) or Medicaid. A few received some allowance from their relatives.

Mike began his practice with these program members by trying to see each of them at least once every two weeks. This was difficult, especially considering their transportation problems and, for some, their low motivation for engaging in any kind of professional contact. He also tried scheduling some of them to meet in groups. This did not work well, for the same reasons. He also was not able to provide a group atmosphere or group activities that facilitated group interaction for this population of members.

From his recent educational experiences, he knew about day treatment for the chronically ill but was hesitant to suggest this option to his supervisors. First, it was a very expensive approach, and there simply were no funds in the mental health center's budget to support this type of endeavor. Second, he was aware that traditional day treatment could continue to isolate this group from their community, even if they would be better able to connect with staff and one another.

Therefore Mike decided to develop a community-based case management program and attempt to activate neighborhood resources to support his program members. Most of his membership lived in one of two areas of the city. Mike began visiting the churches in these areas, meeting with pastors and church members, carefully judging their interest in helping their neighbors with chronic mental disorders. In these discussions, he mentioned the need for a community center where these neighbors could meet, participate in activities with one another and their neighbors, and also have contact with their case manager and their prescribing psychiatrists. At the same time, he was also looking at the physical plant at each church to see if it could handle thirty to forty people twice a week and what it might cost to use that space. During this community assessment period, Mike was also negotiating with the mental health center administrators to see how much money might be made available to support this community approach and whether any other staff, besides himself, could be assigned to this project.

Mike was able to find two churches with the appropriate available space whose pastors and lay governing boards seemed interested in the project. The mental health center decided to give Mike a budget of two thousand dollars a month, another full-time mental health associate to support this endeavor, and the use of two cell phones. Mike offered each church five hundred dollars per month to cover the cost of using their space from noon to three p.m. twice a week. The rest of the funds were budgeted for program supplies to support activities.

Once these agreements with the mental health center and the two churches were solidified, Mike began presenting his plans to both church congregations and to other community organizations nearby, including community service groups. He asked that they support this community program in one or more of the following ways: volunteer their time to participate in the program, become a mentor to one of the program members, or donate money to help support the program. He was able to develop a cadre of forty volunteer mentors, to whom he immediately offered ongoing weekly group sessions for volunteer training.

Each volunteer mentor was assigned to one program member. Each program member was informed of the program in a personal interview with Mike and then introduced to his or her volunteer mentor. Transportation arrangements were made, if necessary, so that each member could attend one of the church sites. Mike made it clear to the members that only by coming to the church could they talk to their psychiatrists and receive their medications; he also let them know that, except in emergencies, the only way they could connect with him or the other staff member assigned to this project was to attend the activities at the church. Many of the members liked talking to Mike, so this was a motivation for them.

A planning group of volunteers and program members designed the activities that were planned at the two churches. These activities included some traditional arts and crafts projects, but many other types of activities were also planned. Day trips, shopping trips, discussion groups, recreation, entertainment, meal planning and preparation, life skills activities, job interview training, anger management, social skills activities, games, and, of course, snack preparation and consumption were all part of the meetings.

Other activities also began to emerge, sponsored by the volunteer mentors. Some volunteers began inviting their mentees to activities on days when the program was not operating. These activities included lunches and dinners out, movies or shows, community events, church activities, grocery shopping, trips to the mall, and general shopping. Sometimes these activities involved a number of volunteers and members; sometimes they were just one-on-one. It became apparent over time that friendships were forming between some of the volunteers and the program members. In some cases, when members became involved with other community activities, they made new friends, who then invited them to more activities.

Mike was not on the sidelines during the regular program times or when volunteers invited members to outside activities. During program periods, Mike or his assistant was always in attendance. Incidents did occur, but one of the professional staff was always there to support members and volunteers and to model problem solving strategies. In addition, Mike kept facilitating the weekly volunteer meetings. These group meetings became not only a way for Mike to process events with the volunteers and make plans for their future contact with members, but also a social group for the volunteers.

Whenever volunteers wanted to make contact with members outside the regular program times, Mike asked that they let him know in advance. He also let the volunteers know that he was available by cell phone if any problems arose. In many instances, it became clear that this notification was not needed, but Mike and his assistant were always on call. There were very few situations where problems arose.

Mike left this job for one in another state two years after the start of the program. Someone else was hired in his place to continue this community-based case management project. When Mike returned for a visit three years later, the programs in the two churches were still going on. In fact, two more churches had been added in other parts of the city, and the mental health center had significantly increased the budgets for all four sites.

For the Teacher or Trainer
Optional Exercises for Chapter 9

1. Impediments to seeking help

Ask students to imagine that they have some type of problem that they cannot handle themselves, such as one involving drugs or alcohol; couple, marital, or family problems; or anxiety or depression. They know from their training that they need professional help to solve the problem . Ask them what their difficulties would be in seeking help. Would they be different based on the type of problem? Would they include having a label, a societal or family stigma, financial issues, fear of public exposure, etc.? Ask them to form small groups for discussion, report to the class, and lead a class discussion.

2. Ethical implications of integrated case management systems

This exercise can be done in a class discussion, small group discussion, or debate format. Present this scenario to the class: You are part of a successful integrated case management system where your program members who are suffering from an addiction have excellent access to the community's only thirty-day inpatient treatment program. The director of your agency was able to successfully negotiate access to most of the thirty-day slots at this treatment center by promising to augment their payments for thirty days of inpatient treatment with a special foundation grant that he received. After working in this integrated collaboration of agencies for a while, you realize that addicted neighbors who have entered case management systems in other community agencies are not able to get into this thirty-day treatment program, mainly because the program members from your agency are using most of the thirty-day slots. Do you have any professional obligation to all of those addicted neighbors in this community who are not able to access the thirty-day inpatient treatment? If no, why? If yes, why? In either situation, what could or should be done?

3. Cost-containment vs. client-driven case management

Ask students to form small groups of at least four and then divide into two subgroups. Ask them to debate the following proposition, with one subgroup arguing pro and the other arguing con: In a case management program, it is better to see as many neighbors with problems as possible, even if they receive only minimal services, than to restrict the number that can receive services, even if seeing fewer neighbors will mean potentially better outcomes for those who do receive services.

As in any debate, the students on each side should argue their position as effectively as possible, even if they don't believe it. After the debate, ask the students as a class what issues came up for them and how they feel about the outcomes of their debates. There is no right or wrong answer in this debate, which is central to case management services in every community.

References

Allen, M. (1991). Why Are We Talking About Case Management Again? In *Empowering Families: Papers from the Fourth Annual Conference on Family Based Services.* Riverdale, IL: National Association for Family Based Services.

Allen, S. (2003). *Meeting the Needs of Families with At-Risk Infants and Toddlers: Service Coordination Practices in Home Visiting Programs.* Unpublished doctoral dissertation, Indiana State University, Terre Haute.

American Association on Mental Retardation (1992). *Mental Retardation: Definition, Classification and Systems of Support* (9th ed.). Washington, D.C.: American Association on Mental Retardation.

American Association on Mental Retardation (1994). *Position Statement on Case Management/Service Coordination.* Washington, D.C.: Author.

Austin, C. D. (1990). Case Management: Myths and Realities. *Families in Society: The Journal of Contemporary Human Services, 71*(7), 398–405.

Austin, C. D. (1993). Case Management: A Systems Perspective. *Families in Society: The Journal of Contemporary Human Services, 74*(3), 451–459.

Bachrach, L. L. (1989). Case Management: Toward a Shared Definition. *Hospital and Community Psychiatry, 40,* 883–884.

Baerwald, A. (1983). Case Management: Defining a Concept. In L. Wikler & M. Keenan (Eds.), *Developmental Disabilities: No Longer a Private Tragedy.* Silver Spring, MD: National Association of Social Workers and American Association on Mental Deficiency.

Bagarozzi, D., & Kurtz, L. (1983). Administrators' Perspectives on Case Management. *Arete, 8,* 13–21.

Ballew, J. R., & Mink, G. (1997). *Case Management in Social Work: Developing the Professional Skills Needed for Work with Multiproblem Client.* (2nd ed.). Springfield, IL: Charles C. Thomas.

Bardfield, S., Beck-Black, R., Breitner, W., Johnson, D., Mc-Gowan, B., Berman-Rossi, T., Seitzman, B., Shulman, L., Woodrow, R., & Young, A.T. (1991). *Social Work Practice with Maternal and Child Health Populations at Risk.* New York: Columbia University School of Social Work.

Belcher, J. R. (1993). The Trade-offs of Developing a Case Management Model for Chronically Mentally Ill People. *Health and Social Work, 18*(1), 20–21.

Berkowitz, G., Halfon, N., & Klee, L. (1992). Improving Access to Health Care: Case Management for Vulnerable Children. *Social Work in Health Care, 17,* 101–123.

Berger, C. S. (2002). Social Work Case Management in Medical Settings. In A. R. Roberts and G. J. Greene (Eds.). *Social Workers' Desk Reference* (pp.497–501). New York: Oxford University Press.

Bertsche, A., & Horejsi, C. (1980). Coordination of Client Services. *Social Work, 25*(2), 94–98.

Biegel, D. E., Tracy, E. M., & Corvo, K. N. (1994). Strengthening Social Networks: Intervention Strategies for Mental Health Case Managers. *Health and Social Work, 19*(3), 206–216.

Bond, G., Miller, L., Krumwied, R., & Ward, R. (1988). Assertive Case Management in Three CMHSs: A Controlled Study. *Hospital and Community Psychiatry, 39,* 411–418.

Borland, A., McRae, J., & Lycan, C. (1989). Outcomes of Five Years of Continuous Intensive Case Management. *Hospital and Community Psychiatry, 40,* 369–376.

Brannigan, V. M. (1992). Protecting the Privacy of Patient Information in Clinical Networks: Regulatory Effectiveness Analysis. *Annals of the New York Academy of Sciences, 670,* 190–201.

Bush, C. T., Langford, M. W., Rosen, P., & Gott, W. (1990). Operation Outreach: Intensive Case Management for Severely Psychiatrically Disabled Adults. *Hospital and Community Psychiatry, 41,* 647–649.

Case Management Society of America (1998). *Standards of Practice for Case Management.* Little Rock, AR: Author.

Cambridge, P. (1992). Case Management in Community Services: Organizational Responses. *British Journal of Social Work, 22,* 495–517.

Cesta, T. G., & Tahan, H. A. (2003). *The Case Manager's Survival Guide: Winning Strategies for Clinical Practice* (2nd ed.). New York: Mosby.

Chernesky, R. H., & Grube, B. (1999). HIV/AIDS Case Management: Views from the Frontline. *The Care Management Journals, 1*(1), 19–28.

Chernesky, R. H., & Grube, B. (2000). Examining the HIV/AIDS Case Management Process. *Health & Social Work, 25*(4), 243–253.

Coffey, D. S. (2003). Connection and Autonomy in the Case Management Relationship. *Psychiatric Rehabilitation Journal, 26*(4), 404–412.

Cohen, E. L., & DeBank, V. (1999). *The Outcome Mandate: Case Management in Health Care Today.* New York: Mosby.

Cohen, J. A. (2003) Managed Care and the Evolving Role of the Clinical Social Worker in Mental Health. *Social Work, 48*(1), 34–43.

Corcoran, K., & Vandiver, V. (1996). *Maneuvering the Maze of Managed Care: Skills for Mental Health Practitioners.* New York: Free Press.

Cote, G. (2003). A Probation and Parole Service Delivery Model: The Ontario Experience. *Corrections Today, 65*(1), 60–63.

Davidson, J. R., & Davidson, R. (1996). Confidentiality and Managed Care: Ethical and Legal Concerns. *Health and Social Work, 21*(3), 208–215.

Degen, K., Cole, N., Tamayo, L., & Dzerovych, G. (1990). Intensive Case Management for the Seriously Mentally Ill. *Administration and Policy in Mental Health, 17*(4), 265–269.

DeLeon, G. (2000). *The Therapeutic Community: Theory, Model, and Method.* New York: Springer Publishing Company.

DeLeon, G. (2001). *Intregated Systems Approach (ISA): Recovery-based treatment.* Paper presenteed at the 8th European Conference on Rehabilitation and Drug Policy, "21st Century, New Spiritual and Ethical Challenges in Prevention, Treatment, and Research," Sept. 5–8, 2001, Warsaw, Poland.

Dinerman, M. (1992). Managing the Maze: Case Management and Service Delivery. *Administration in Social Work, 16,* 1–9.

Dubler, N. N. (1992). Individual Advocacy as a Governing Principle. *Journal of Case Management, 1,* 82–86.

Dziegielewski, S. (1998). *The Changing Face of Health Care Social Work: Professional Practice in the Era of Managed Care.* New York: Springer Publishing Company.

Edinburg, G., & Cottler, J. (1990). Implications of Managed Care for Social Work in Psychiatric Hospitals. *Hospital and Community Psychiatry, 41,* 1063–1064.

Edinburg, G., & Cottler, J. (1995). Managed Care. In R.L. Edwards (Ed.), *Encyclopedia of Social Work* (19th ed., pp. 1635–1642). Washington, D.C.: NASW Press.

Eggert, G., Friedman, B., & Zimmer, J. (1990). Models of Intensive Case Management. *Journal of Gerontological Social Work, 15,* 75–101.

Emlet, C. A. & Gusz, S. S. (1998). Service Use Patterns in HIV/AIDS Case Management: A Five-year Study. *Journal of Case Management, 7*(1), 3–9.

Feine, J., & Taylor, P. (1991). Serving Rural Families of Developmentally Disabled Children: A Case Management Model. *Social Work, 36*(4), 323–327.

Frank, R., & McGuire, T. (1986). A Review of Studies of the Impact of Insurance on Demand and Utilization of Specialty Mental Health Services. *Health Services Research, 21,* 241–265.

Frankel, A. J., & LaPorte, H. H. (1998). Tracking Case Management: A Systems Approach. *Journal of Case Management, 3*(7), 105–112 .

Frankel, A. J. (1999). The Evaluation of a Successful Community-Based Program for Forensic MICA Clients. *Justice Professional, 11*(4) 21–30.

Frankel, A. J., White, T., Walzer, J., Lamon, S., & McAuliffe, N.

(1998). The Evaluation of a Successful Community-Based Program for Forensic MICA Clients, *The Justice Professional,* 11(4), 423-436.

Franklin, C. (2002). Developing Effective Practice Competencies in Managed Behavioral Health Care. In A.R. Roberts and G.J. Greene (Eds). *Social Workers' Desk Reference* (pp. 3–10). New York: Oxford University Press.

Gelman, S. (1974). A System of Services. In C. Cherington and G. Dybwad (Eds.), *New Neighbors: The Retarded Children in Quest of a Home* (pp. 91–103). Washington, D.C.: President's Committee on Mental Retardation.

Gelman, S. (1983). The Developmentally Disabled: A Social Work Challenge. In L. Wikler and M. Keenan (Eds.), *Developmental Disabilities: No Longer a Private Charity* (pp. 12–14). Silver Spring, MD: National Association of Social Workers and American Association on Mental Deficiency.

Gelman, S. (1989). Advocacy: Working toward Positive Change. In J.M. Levy, P.H. Levy, & B. Niven, *Strengthening Families* (pp. 234–327). New York: Young Adult Institute Press.

Gelman, S. (1991). Client Access to Agency Records: A Comparative Analysis. *International Social Work, 34,* 191–204.

Gelman, S. (1992). Risk Management through Client Access to Case Records. *Social Work, 37*(1), 73–79.

Gibelman, M. (2002). Social Work in an Era of Managed Care. In A. R. Roberts and G. J. Greene (Eds). *Social Workers' Desk Reference* (pp. 16–23). New York: Oxford University Press.

Giddens, B., Káopua, L. S., & Tomaszewski, E. P. (2002). HIV/AIDS Case Management. In A. R. Roberts and G. J. Greene (Eds). *Social Workers' Desk Reference* (pp. 506–510). New York: Oxford University Press.

Gilson, S. F.(1998). Case Management and Supported Employment. *Journal of Case Management, 7*(1), 10–17.

Grossman, A. H., & Silverstein, C. (1993). Facilitating Support Groups For Professionals Working With AIDS. *Social Work, 38*(2), 144–151.

Grube, B. & Chernesky, R. H. (2001). What do Case Managers do? The Results of a Functional Analysis Study. *Social Work in Health Care, 32*(3), 41–64.

Hagen, J. L. (1994). Jobs and Case Management: Developments in 10 States. *Social Work, 39*(2), 197–205.

Hall, J. A., Carswell, C., Walsh, E., Huber, D. L., & Jampoler, J. S. (2002). Iowa Case Management: Innovative Social Casework, *Social Work, 47*(2), 132–141.

Hanley, B., & Parkinson, C. (1994). Position Paper on Social Work Values: Practice with Individuals Who Have Developmental Disabilities. *Mental Retardation, 32*(6), 426–431.

Hegar, R. L. (1992). Monitoring Child Welfare Services. In B. S. Vourlekis & R. R. Greene (Eds.), *Social Work Case Management* (pp. 135– 148). New York: Aldine DeGruyter.

Heslin, K. C., Anderson, R. M., & Gelberg, L. (2003). Case Management and Access to Services for Homeless Women. *Journal of Health Care for the Poor and Understanding, 14*(1), 34–51.

Hiratsuka, J. (1990). Managed Care: A Sea of Change in Health. *NASW NEWS, 35,* 3.

Horejsi, C. (1979). Developmental Disabilities: Opportunities for Social Workers. *Social Work, 24*(1), 40–43.

Indyk, D., Belville, R., Lachapelle, S., Gordon, G., & Dewart, T. (1993). A Community-based Approach to HIV Case Management: Systematizing the Unmanageable. *Social Work, 38*(4), 380–387.

Itagliata, J. (1982). Improving the Quality of Care for Chronically Mentally Disabled: The Role of Case Management. *Schizophrenia Bulletin, 8,* 655–674.

Jackson, V. H. (1995). *Managed Care Resource Guide for Social Workers in Agency Settings.* Washington, D.C.: NASW Press.

Jansson, B. S. (2003). *Becoming an Effective Policy Advocate: From Practice to Social Justice* (4th ed.). Pacific Grove, CA: Brooks/Cole.

Johnson, P., & Rubin, A. (1983). Case Management in Mental Health: A Social Work Domain. *Social Work, 28*(1), 49–55.

Kagel, J. (1993). Record keeping: Directions for the 1990s. *Social Work, 38*(2), 190–196.

Kane, R. A. (1992). Case Management in Long-Term Care: It Can Be Ethical and Efficacious. *Journal of Case Management, 1,* 76–81.

Kane, R. A., & Caplan, A.L. (1992). *Ethical Conflicts in Management Home Care: The Case Manager's Dilemma.* New York: Springer Publishing Company.

Kanter, J. (1987). Mental Health Case Management: A Professional Domain? *Social Work, 32*(5), 461–462.

Kanter, J. (1989). Clinical Case Management: Definitions, Principles, Components. *Hospital and Community Psychiatry, 40,* 361–368.

Kanter, J. (1991). Integrating Case Management and Psychiatric Hospitalization. *Health and Social Work, 16*(1), 34–42.

Kaplan, K. (1992). Linking the Developmentally Disabled Client to Needed Resources: Adult Protective Services Case Management. In B. S. Vourlekis & R. R. Greene (Eds.), *Social Work Case Management* (pp. 89–106). New York: Aldine DeGruyter.

Kaplan, M. (1992). Case Planning for Children with HIV/AIDS: A Family Perspective. In B. S. Vourlekis & R. R. Greene (Eds.), *Social Work Case Management* (pp. 75–88). New York: Aldine DeGruyter.

Kisthardt, W., & Rapp, C. (1992). Bridging the Gap between Principles and Practice: Implementing a Strengths Perspective. In S. M. Rose (Ed.), *Case Management and Social Work* (pp.112–125). New York: Longman.

Lamb, H. (1980). Therapist-case Managers: More than Brokers of Services. *Hospital and Community Psychiatry, 31,* 762–764.

LaPorte, H. H., & Frankel, A. J. (2000). Computer-assisted Tracking of A Case Management Program for the Homeless. *The Case Management Journals, 2*(3), 153–159.

Lawrence, L. M. (1994). Safeguarding the Confidentiality of Automated Medical Information. *The Joint Commission Journal on Quality Improvement, 20*(1), 639–646.

Lebow, G., & Kane, B. (1992). Assessment: Private Case Management with the Elderly. In B. S. Vourlekis & R. R. Greene (Eds.), *Social Work Case Management* (pp. 35–50). New York: Aldine DeGruyter.

Levine, I., & Fleming, M. (1985). *Human Resource Development: Issues in Case Management.* College Park, MD: Center for Rehabilitation and Manpower Services.

Liou, K. T. (1997). Employee Job Stress in the AIDS Service Organization: A Study of Personal and Job Factors. *The Journal of Health and Human Services Association, 20*(2), 242–253.

Litwak, E. (1985). *Helping the Family: The Complementary Role of Informal Networks and Formal Systems.* New York: Guilford Press.

Loomis, J. (1988). Case Management Is Health Care. *Health and Social Work, 13*(3), 219–225.

Marcendo, M. O., & Smith, L. K. (1992). The Impact of a Family-Centered Case Management Approach. *Social Work in Health Care, 17*(1), 87–100.

Mason, S. E., & Siris, S. G. (1992). Dual Diagnosis: The Case for Case Management. *The American Journal of Addictions, 1,* 77–82.

Mather, J. H., & Hull, G. H. (2002). Case Management and Child Welfare. In A. R. Roberts & G. J. Greene (Eds.). *Social Workers' Desk Reference* (pp. 476–480). New York: Oxford University Press.

Miller, N. (1992). Plan Implementation and Coordination: Case Management in an Employee Assistance Program. In B. S. Vourlekis & R. R. Greene (Eds.), *Social Work Case Management* (125–134). New York: Aldine DeGruyter.

Mills-Groninger, T. (2003, May 1). Change Management in Case Management: Issues in Automating Client Tracking and Outcome Measures. *Non-profit Times,* 19–21.

Mizrahi, R. (1993). Managed Care and Managed Competition: A Primer for Social Work. *Health and Social Work, 18*(2), 86–91.

Moore, S. (1987). The Capacity to Care: A Family Focused Approach to Social Work Practice with the Disabled Elderly. *Journal of Gerontological Social Work, 10,* 79–99.

Moore, S. (1990). A Social Work Practice Model of Case Management: The Case Management Grid. *Social Work, 35*(5), 444–448.

Moore, S. (1992). Case Management and the Integration of Services: How Service Delivery Systems Shape Case Management. *Social Work, 37*(5), 418–423.

Morrow-Howell, N. (1992). Clinical Case Management: The Hallmark of Gerontological Social Work. *Journal of Gerontological Social Work, 18,* 119–131.

Morrow-Howell, N. (1992b). Clinical Case Management: Service or Symptom? *Social Work, 37*(2), 160–164.

Moxley, D. P. (1989). *The Practice of Case Management.* Thousand Oaks, CA: Sage Publications.

Moxley, D. P. (1997). *Case Management by Design.* Chicago: Nelson-Hall.

Moxley, D. P. (2002). Case Management and Psychosocial Rehabilitation with SMD Clients. In A. R. Roberts & G. J. Greene (Eds). *Social Workers' Desk Reference* (pp.481–485). New York: Oxford University Press.

National Association of Social Workers (1984). *NASW Standards and Guidelines for Social Work Case Management for the Functionally Impaired.* Silver Spring, MD: Author.

National Association of Social Workers (1992). *Standards for Social Work Case Management.* Washington, D.C.: Author.

National Association of Social Workers (1993). *The Social Work Perspective on Managed Care for Mental Health and Substance Abuse Treatment.*Washington, D.C.: Author.

National Association of Social Workers (1996). *Code of Ethics.* Washington, D.C.: Author.

National Conference on Social Welfare (1981). *Case Management: State of the Art.* Washington, D.C.: Author.

Nelson, G. (1982). Support for the Aged: Public and Private Responsibility. *Social Work, 27*(2), 137–143.

New York City Task Force on Managed Care in Child Welfare (1996). *Implementation of Managed Care in Child Welfare: Issues to Consider.* New York: Federation of Protestant Welfare Agencies/Children's Defense Fund.

O'Connor, G. (1988). Case Management: System and Practice. *Social Casework, 69*(2), 97–106.

Perloff, J. (1996). Medicaid Managed Care and Urban Poor People: Implications for Social Work. *Health and Social Work, 21*(3), 189–195.

President's Panel on Mental Retardation (1962). *National Action to Combat Mental Retardation.* Washington, D.C.: Superintendent of Documents.

Quinn, J. (1993). *Successful Case Management in Long-Term Care.* New York: Springer Publishing Company.

Raiff, N. R., & Shore, B. K. (1993). *Advanced Case Management.* Thousand Oaks, CA: Sage Publications.

Rapp, C., & Chamberlain, R. (1985). Case Management Services for the Chronically Mentally Ill. *Social Work, 30*(5), 417–422.

Rapp, C. (1997). The Strengths Perspective and Persons with Substance Abuse Problems. In D. Saleebey (Ed.) *The Strengths Perspective in Social Work Practice* (pp. 77–96). New York: Longman.

Rapp, C. A. (2002). A Strengths Approach to Case Management with Clients with Sever Mental Disabilities. In A. R. Roberts & G. J. Greene (Eds.) *Social Workers' Desk Reference* (pp. 486–489). New York: Oxford University Press.

Rife, J., First, R., Greenlee, R., Miller, L., & Feichter, M. (1991). Case Management Services with Homeless, Mentally Ill People. *Health and Social Work, 16*(1), 58–67.

Roberts, C., Severinsen, C., Kuehn, C., Straker, D., & Fritz, C. (1992). Obstacles to Effective Case Management with AIDS Patients: The Clinician's Perspective. *Social Work in Health Care, 17,* 27–40.

Rose, S. (1992). *Case Management and Social Work Practice.* New York: Longman.

Rose, S., & Moore, J. (1995). Case Management. In R. Edwards (Ed.), *Encyclopedia of Social Work* (19th ed., pp. 335–340). Washington, D.C.: NASW Press.

Rothman, J. (1991). A Model of Case Management: Toward Empirically Based Practice. *Social Work, 36*(6), 520–528.

Rothman, J. (1994). *Practice with Highly Vulnerable Clients: Case Management and Community-Based Service.* Englewood Cliffs, NJ: Prentice Hall.

Rothman, J., & Sager, J. S. (Eds.) (1998). *Case Management: Integrating Individual and Community Practice.* (2nd ed.). Boston: Allyn and Bacon.

Rothman, J. (2002). An Overview of Case Management. In A. R.

Roberts & G. J. Greene (Eds.) *Social Workers' Desk Reference*, (pp. 467–472). New York: Oxford University Press.

Rubin, A. (1992). Case Management. In S. M. Rose (Ed.) *Case Management and Social Work Practice* (pp.5–20). New York: Longman.

Rubin, A. (1992). Is Case Management Effective for People with Serious Mental Illness? A Research Review. *Health and Social Work, 17*(2), 138–150.

Ryan, C. S., & Sherman, P. S. (1994). Accounting for Case Manager Effects in the Evaluation of Mental Health Services. *Journal of Consulting and Clinical Psychology, 62*(5), 965–974.

Saleeby, D. (1992). *The Strengths Perspective in Social Work Practice.* New York: Longman.

Saleebey, D. (Ed.) (1997). *The Strengths Perspective in Social Work Practice.* New York: Longman.

Scannapieco, M., & Hegar, R. L. (1994). Kinship Care: Two Case Management Models. *Child and Adolescent Social Work, 11*(4), 315–324.

Schalock, R. L. (1996). *Quality of Life: Conceptualization and Measurement.* Washington, D.C.: American Association on Mental Retardation.

Schamess, G., & Lightburn, A. (1998). *Humane Managed Care?* Washington, DC: NASW Press.

Schilling, R., Schinke, S., & Weatherly, R. (1988). Service Trends in a Conservative Era: Social Workers Rediscover the Past. *Social Work, 33*(1), 5–10.

Schoen, K. (1998). Caregiving for Ourselves: Understanding and Minimizing the Stress of HIV Caregiving. In D. M. Aronstein & B. J. Thompson (Eds). *HIV and Social Work: A Practitioner's Guide* (pp.527–536). New York: The Haworth Press.

Sederer, L. I., & St. Clair, R. I. (1990). Quality Assurance and Managed Care. *Psychiatric Clinics of North America, 13,* 89–97.

Seltzer, M., Ivry, J., & Litchfield, L. (1987). Family Members as Case Managers: Partnership between the Formal and Informal Support Networks. *The Gerontologist, 27,* 722–728.

Seltzer, M., Litchfield, L., Kapust, L., & Mayer, J. (1992). Professional and Family Collaboration in Case Management. *Social Work in Health Care, 17,* 1–22.

Seltzer, M., Wyngaarden Krauss, M., & Janicki, M. (1996). *Life Course Perspectives on Adulthood and Old Age.* Washington, D.C.: American Association on Mental Retardation.

Shera, W. (1996). Managed Care and People with Severe Mental Illness: Challenges and Opportunities for Social Work. *Health and Social Work, 21*(3), 196–201.

Shorter, B. D. (1990). Managed Care/Case Management: What, Why, and How to Cope. *Discharge Planning Update, 10,* 1–19.

Siegal, H. A., & Rapp, R. C. (1996). *Case Management and Substance Abuse.* New York: Springer Publishing Company.

Siegal, H. A., Li, L., & Rapp, R. C.(2002). Case Management as a Therapeutic Enhancement: Impact on Post-Treatment Criminality. *Journal of Addictive Diseases, 21*(4), 37–46.

Simmons, K., Ivry, J., & Seltzer, M. (1985). Agency-Family Collaboration. *Practice Concepts, 25,* 343–346.

Snowden, F. (Ed.) (2003). *Case Manager's Desk Reference.* Gaithersburg, MD: Aspen Publishers.

Soares, H., & Rose, M. (1994). Clinical Aspects of Case Management with the Elderly. *Journal of Gerontological Social Work, 22*(3/4), 143–156.

Solomon, P., & Draine, J. (1995). Jail Recidivism in a Forensic Case Management Program. *Health and Social Work, 20*(3), 167–173.

Standards for Privacy of Individually Identifiable Health Information (2003). Available at http://www.hhs.gov/ocr/hipaa.

Stein, T., Gambrill, E., & Wiltse, K. (1977). Dividing Case Management in Foster Family Cases. *Child Welfare, 56*(5), 321–331.

Strom-Gottfried, K. (1996). The Implications of Managed Care for Social Work Education. *Journal of Social Work Education, 33*(1), 7–18.

Strug, D., & Podell, C. (2002). A Bereavement Support Group for Pediatric HIV/AIDS Case Managers and Social Workers: Helping Members Cope with Dying Children. *Social Work with Groups, 25*(3), 61–75.

Sullivan, W., Wolk, J., & Hartmann, D. (1992). Case Management in Alcohol and Drug Treatment: Improving Client Outcomes. *Families in Society: The Journal of Contemporary Human Services, 73*(3), 195–204.

Sullivan, W. P., & Fisher, B. J. (1994). Intervening for Success: Strength-based Case Management and Successful Aging. *Journal of Gerontological Social Work, 22,* 61–74.

Sullivan, W., Hartmann, D. J., Dillon, D., & Wolk, J. L. (1994). Implementing Case Management in Alcohol and Drug Treatment. *Families in Society: The Journal of Contemporary Human Services, 75*(2), 67–73.

Sullivan, W. P. (2002). Case Management with Substance-Abusing Clients. In A. R. Roberts & G. J. Greene (Eds.) *Social Workers' Desk Reference,* (pp. 467–472). New York: Oxford University Press.

Thompson, B. J. (1998). Case Management in AIDS Service Settings. In D. D. Aronstein & B. J. Thompson (Eds.) *HIV and Social Work: A Practitioner's Guide,* (pp. 75–87). New York: The Haworth Press.

Tice, C., & Perkins, K. (1998). Case Management for the Baby Boom Generation: A Strengths Perspective. *Journal of Case Management, 7*(1), 31–36.

Vourlekis, B. S., & Greene, R. R. (Eds.) (1992). *Social Work Case Management.* New York: Aldine DeGruyter.

Wade, K., & Simon, E.P. (1993). Survival Bonding: A Response to Stress and Work with AIDS. *Social Work in Health Care, 19*(1), 77–89.

Walsh, J. (2002). Clinical Case Management. In A. R. Roberts & G. J. Greene (Eds.) *Social Workers' Desk Reference,* (pp. 472–476). New York: Oxford University Press.

Watkins, S. A. (1989). Confidentiality and Privileged Information: Legal Dilemma for Family Therapists. *Social Work, 34*(2), 133–136.

Wehmeyer, M., & Metzler, C. (1995). How Self-Determined Are People with Mental Retardation? The National Consumer Survey. *Mental Retardation, 33*(2), 111–119.

Weick, A., Rapp, C., Sullivan, W., & Kisthardt, W. (1989). A Strengths Perspective for Social Work Practice. *Social Work, 34*(4), 350–354.

Weil, M., & Karls, J. (1985). *Case Management in Human Services Practice.* San Francisco: Jossey Bass.

Werrbach, G. B. (1994). Intensive Case Management: Work Roles and Activities. *Child and Adolescent Social Work Journal, 11*(4), 325–341.

Werrbach, G. B. (2002). Providing Intensive Child Case Management Services? How do Case Managers Spend Their Time? *Child & Adolescent Social Work Journal, 19*(6), 473–486.

Whaley, D. C., & Malott, R. W. (1996). *Elementary Principles of Behavior.* New York: Appleton-Century-Croft.

Winegar, N. (1996). *The Clinician's Guide to Managed Behavioral Care* (2nd ed.). New York: The Haworth Press.

Wolk, J., Sullivan, W., & Hartmann, D. (1994). The Managerial Nature of Case Management. *Social Work, 39*(2), 152–159.

Yarmo, D. (1998). Research Directions for Case Management. *Journal of Case Management, 7*(2), 84–91.

Case Management Source Guide

With *Elderly Clients*
 Austin and McClelland, 2002
 Eggert, Friedman, and Zimmer, 1990
 Kane, 1992
 Kane and Caplan, 1992
 Lebow and Kane, 1992
 Quinn, 1993
 Soares and Rose, 1994
 Sullivan and Fisher, 1994

With *Substance Abusers*
 Hall et al., 2002
 Mason and Siris, 1992
 Morrow-Howell, 1992
 Nelson, 1982
 Rapp, 1997
 Siegel and Rapp, 1996
 Sullivan, 2002
 Sullivan, Wolk, and Hartmann, 1992
 Sullivan, Hartmann, Dillon, and Wolk, 1994

With the *Chronically Mentally Ill*
 Belcher, 1993
 Bond et al., 1988
 Bush et al., 1990
 Cohen, 2003
 Degen et al., 1990
 Frankel et al., 1998
 Johnson and Rubin, 1983
 Kanter, 1987 and 1991

Moxley, 2002
Rapp, 2002
Rapp and Chamberlain, 1985
Rubin, 1992
Rife et al., 1991
Shera, 1996

With *the Homeless*
Heslin et al., 2003
LaPorte and Frankel, 2000

With *Developmentally Disabled Individuals*
Allen, 2003
American Association on Mental Retardation, 1994
Baerwald, 1983
Feine and Taylor, 1991
Hanley and Parkinson, 1994
Horejsi, 1979
Kaplan, K., 1992

With *AIDS Patients*
Chernesky and Grube, 1999, 2000
Emlet and Gusz, 1998
Giddens et al., 2002
Indyk et al., 1993
Kaplan, M., 1992
Roberts et al., 1992
Siegal and Rapp, 1996
Strug and Podell, 2002
Thompson, 1998

In the *Criminal Justice System*
Cote, 2003
Frankel, 1999
Frankel et al., 1998
Siegal et al., 2002
Solomon and Draine, 1995

In *Child Welfare*
Hegar, 1992
Mather and Hill, 2002

Stein, Gambrill, and Wiltse, 1977
Werrbach, 2002

With *Families*
Allen, 1991
Berkowitz, Halfon, and Klee, 1992
Litwak, 1985
Loomis, 1988
Marcendo and Smith, 1992
Moore, 1987
Scannapieco and Hegar, 1994
Seltzer, Ivry, and Litchfield, 1987
Seltzer et al., 1992
Simmons, Ivry, and Seltzer, 1985
Werrbach, 2002

In *Employment Training and Employment Assistance Programs*
Gilson, 1998
Hagen, 1994
Miller, 1992

With *Other Populations at Risk*
Ballew and Mink, 1997
Bardfield et al., 1991
Vourlekis and Greene, 1992

In *Health Care*
Berger, 2002
Cohen, 1999
Dziegielewski, 1998

Index